EDITOR: MARTIN

OSPREY
MILITARY

MEN-AT-ARM

GERMAN C
EQUIPMENTS 1939-45

CW00920862

Text by
GORDON L. ROTTMAN
Colour plates by
RON VOLSTAD

Published in 1991 by
Osprey Publishing Ltd
59 Grosvenor Street, London W1X 9DA
© Copyright 1991 Osprey Publishing Ltd

British Library Cataloguing in Publication Data
Rottman, Gordon L.
    German combat equipments 1939–45. – (Men-at-
arms series, 234).
    1. Germany. Heer. Infantry. Military
equipment. Weapons, history
I. Title   II. Series
623.40943

    ISBN 0-85045-952-4

Filmset in Great Britain
Printed through Bookbuilders Ltd, Hong Kong

Acknowledgements

I greatly appreciate the assistance and information
provided by Paul Lemmer, Marvin Schroder, Ron
Volstad, and Martin Windrow. A very special thanks
goes to Jim Cummingham and Troy Haley who so
willingly opened their collections and shared their
knowledge. I wish also to thank my wife, Enriqueta,
for her assistance with the material related
terminology.

Artist's Note

Readers may care to note that the original paintings
from which the colour plates in this book were
prepared are available for private sale. All
reproduction copyright whatsoever is retained by the
publisher. All enquiries to be addressed to:
    Ronald B. Volstad
    24 Dixon Crescent
    Red Deer
    Alberta
    Canada T4R 2J1
The publishers regret that they can enter into no
correspondence upon this matter.

For a catalogue of all books published by Osprey Military
please write to:

**The Marketing Manager,
Consumer Catalogue Department,
Osprey Publishing Ltd,
Michelin House, 81 Fulham Road,
London SW3 6RB**

INTRODUCTION

The goal of this book is not to provide a definitive study (if there is such a thing on any subject) of German military combat equipments in all their many variants and styles. Rather, it will focus on the principal standard items of equipment utilised by the *Heer* (Army) during the war years. However, for the most part this same or very similar equipment was used by the other branches of the *Wehrmacht* (Defence Forces): ground troops of the *Luftwaffe* and *Kriegsmarine*, and the *Waffen-SS*. Equipments peculiar to these branches are not the subject of this book[1]. I hope that modellers, collectors, re-enactors, and those interested in general German military topics will find this a useful guide for the identification, wear, and manner in which German field equipment was used. When describing the position in which an equipment item was worn on an individual, it will be from the wearer's viewpoint. When describing the location of a component on an item of equipment, it will be from the viewer's reference.

In order to conduct a conversation, or discuss a military topic, the participants must possess a common vocabulary. I will use somewhat literal translations of German equipment **nomenclatures** rather than attempt to identify items by parallel British or US terms, and to provide a degree of standardisation. The common collectors' terms will be included where appropriate. German model designations were composed of the equipment item's descriptive name followed by the last two digits of the year of adoption, for example '*Tornister 39*' (many items did not include the year). I will use this system when providing the German designation, but in English I will use e.g. the easily understandable 'M1939 pack'.

German combat equipment was of relatively light weight, ruggedly constructed, well designed, functional, and of generally high quality, though deteriorating in the later war years. A high degree of design standardisation was maintained in most categories of equipment, though materials and their colours often varied widely. Its quality did not drastically deteriorate after

1942, as did that of many other types of equipment, though increased use was made of substitute and lower grade materials. In late 1944 an attempt was made to standardise field equipment between all armed services in design, materials and colours as a means of conservation. This universal equipment (*Einheits Ausrüstungsstrüke*) was based on the Army's standard items.

One of the principal **materials** used in combat equipment was leather (*Leder*). It was widely used as the main component of belts, support straps, ammunition pouches, holsters, horse equipment, and the many special purpose pouches, carriers, cases, and packs. Leather was also extensively used as edge binding, securing straps, and reinforcement. Both smooth and pebble finishes were used. Though fairly durable and long lasting if properly maintained, leather does have a number of disadvantages. It is expensive, heavy, stiff, easily cracked when dry and torn when wet, and suffers from shrinkage when drying. In wartime Germany it also became a very scarce commodity.

Cotton canvas (*Baumwolle Segeltuch*) was used extensively in packs, rucksacks, bags, pouches, and special carriers and cases in a wide variety of weights and weaves. Lighter weight canvas of rougher weaves came into use as the war progressed. Other fabrics, used to a lesser degree in some items, included: felt (*Filz*), wool (*Wolle*), rayon (*Kunstseide*, literally—artificial silk), and linen (*Leinen*). The tent quarter was made of water-repellent gabardine (*Gabardine*).

Various types of cotton webbing (*Gurtband*) were used for carrying, securing and reinforcing straps in many items, even prior to the war, though its use increased from 1943. (Some slings and shoulder straps were fabricated using folded and sewn canvas rather than webbing.) Canvas and webbing was also used in the equipment specially designed for use in North Africa, as well as in later items to conserve leather. Cotton, wool, and rayon thread (*Faden*), whether used with canvas, webbing or leather, was normally white, though this soon became stained with use; it was felt, rightly, that dyed thread would be weakened by the process.

Substitute or replacement (*Ersatz*) materials came into wide

[1] For information on these branches' equipment, see MAA 139, *German Airborne Troops 1939–45*, MAA 34, *The Waffen-SS (Revised)*, MAA 229, *Luftwaffe Field Divisions 1939–45*. The reader is also referred to MAA 213, *German Military Police Units 1939–45*.

Early German packs (Tornistern), left to right: M1809, M1867, M1887   ***(back view with belt), and M1895. (Visier)***

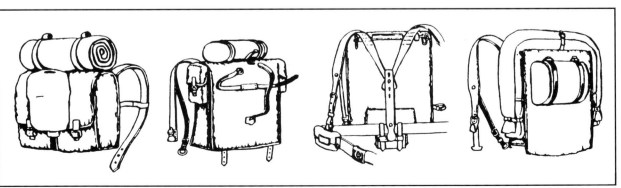

use from about 1943, though these were in limited use prior to and early in the war. The principal of these was a leather-like treated pressed cardboard (*Press-Stoff*, literally—pressed material), used in lieu of leather in items not requiring high durability or load sustainment. Limited use was also made of artificial leather (*Kunstleder*).

Hardware or metal fittings (*Beschlag*) were made of steel (*Stahl*), aluminium (*Aluminium*), and light metal alloy (*Leicht-metall*). Common hardware components, available in many sizes, included: buckle—with tongue (*Schnalle*); slide buckle—friction (*Schiebeschnalle*); slide—oval (*Schieber*); 'O' ring (*Ringe*); 'D' ring (*Halbrunde Ringe*), 'D' ring with hook (*Halbrunde Ringe mit Haken*); carbine hook—spring-loaded snap-hook (*Karbiner-haken*); wire side-hook (*Drahtseitenhaken*); button (*Knöpfe*); and stud (*Dobbelknöpfe*).

Though some hardware was unpainted, generally it was painted field grey or various other shades of grey. In late 1944, as part of the universal standardisation effort, an attempt was made to standardise hardware paint as dark grey within all armed services, though this was only achieved to a limited extent.

Some use was made of synthetic materials. Bakelite (*Bakelit*), a hard heat-treated plastic of various colours, usually cream to brown and black (and non-conductive to electricity), was used as a component in some items. Another synthetic material was a phenolic resin composition, ranging from reddish to dark brown in colour.

There was little standardisation in the **colours** of field equipment materials, especially among canvas/webbing items, and different colours are even encountered in the same item due to material shortages or repairs. When specific colours are listed for a given item, these do not necessarily exhaust the possible colours it may be found in. Field grey was the more common colour (though others were used) prior to and early in the war, but from 1941/42 olive green and other green shades tended to predominate. Later, items were fabricated from whatever colour material stocks were available.

Typical fabric colours included: field grey (*feldgrau*—grey green with the green much more pronounced); olive green (*olivegrün*—deep brownish green); reed green (*schilfgrün*—light dusty green, though it varied greatly from light green to light olive brown); dark and light grey (*dunkel- und hellgrau*); dark and light brown (*dunkel- und hellbraun*); dark and light tan (beige) colour (*dunkel- und hell-lohfarbe*); and sand colour (*sandfarbe*). Even these shades varied widely; and a few other 'odd' colours, described in the text and unique to specific items, will be encountered. Surviving fabric equipment items may have faded considerably or changed in tone due to exposure to the elements, washing, wear, dye deterioration, or a combination of these.

Metal equipment items, such as cook pots, entrenching tools and gas mask cases, were usually painted matt (flat) black (*schwarz*), dull or matt grey (*stumpf-order mattgrau*), field grey, or olive green, the latter being more common from 1941. Some tropical equipment used in North Africa was painted in reed green, sand, and tan shades. Prior to 1943 most large metal items, to include unit equipment, vehicles, ammunition boxes, etc., were painted dark grey (*dunkelgrau P24*—called 'panzer grey' by modellers), though some were painted field grey. Due to green pigment shortages and the need to provide a light base colour so that darker camouflaging colours could be applied, dark yellow (*dunkelgelb*—called 'ordnance tan' by collectors) was adopted in 1943 and applied to most equipment in the factory; dark yellow items were thus not necessarily intended for use in North Africa as is sometimes assumed. The *Luftwaffe* used metal equipment items painted blue grey (*blaugrau*—sometimes incorrectly called 'ordnance blue' by collectors). However, this colour was also used by the Army, particularly for machine gun-related items, late in the war.

Leather items were black, darker shades of brown, or, in remote cases, natural (light) brown or tan. It was not uncommon for both black and brown leather components to be used in the construction of a single item. Stock leather was dyed prior to cutting for fabrication and the raw cut edges and rough inside

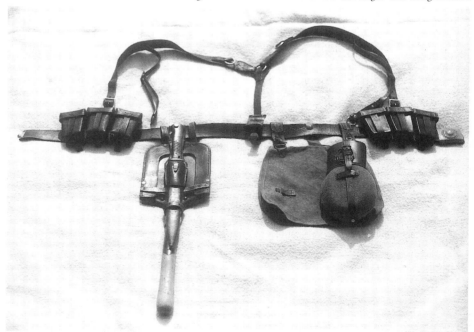

An early infantryman's basic equipment; 'belt supports with auxiliary straps' (redesignated 'belt supports for infantry' in April 1940), belt, M1911 cartridge pouches, small entrenching tool and carrier, S.84/98 bayonet, M1931 bread bag, and M1931 field flask. (Troy Haley collection)

Troops, wearing standard infantry equipment, enter a Polish city after the capitulation. The NCO platoon leader (unit strength authorisation tables prescribed that one platoon leader in each company be an NCO), in the centre and to the left of his platoon, is outfitted with an M1935 report/map case and pistol holster. (Author's collection)

An Armament Office (Waffenamt) acceptance symbol stamped on a tent accessories pouch's leather retaining loop. Many equipment items were 'denazified', after the war by obliterating this symbol causing those with the symbol to be of more value to collectors. Beneath the symbol is the manufacturer's mark (Herstellungszeichen)- 'WSA535'.

were left undyed, though this soon became darkly stained with use. Leather equipment made for officers tended to be *orange-farbe*, a light reddish brown, but darker browns were also used. It was ordered in July 1943 that brown items be dyed black, but this was not always accomplished. Brown and natural leather are found in some tropical equipment, though little used in such items due to its tendency to crack in dry climates. Standard black and dark brown leather items used in North Africa were sometimes painted sand or tan, while on the Continent they were occasionally painted field grey or other green shades. In the winter leather items were sometimes painted white (*weiss*) or whitewashed (*weisstünche*) for snow camouflage.

The **markings** found on German field equipment are of particular interest to collectors. Almost all were stamped in black ink. In 1936 a system of codes was adopted to identify the Army Clothing Office (*Heeresbekleidungsamt*) from which the equipment originated. A single letter was followed by a two-digit year

number, for example 'B 38'. The letters were: B—*Berlin*, E—*Erfurt*, K—*Köningsberg*, M—*München*. With the pre-war expansion of the Army Clothing Offices this system was dropped and only the year was applied. Unit designation abbreviations were also stamped or inked on some items, but this practice was discontinued within the field army after the outbreak of war for security reasons. From 1934 Armament Office (*Waffenamt*) acceptance symbol (a spread-winged eagle clutching a swastika) was impact stamped on most items, as was often 'R.B.' (*Reichs Bekleidung*—National Clothing). Private contractors were usually identified by their trade name and location or a manufacturer's mark (*Herstellungszeichen*) in the form of a lower case three-letter code, though trademark symbols (*Schutzmarke*) with year of manufacture were also common.

5

DEVELOPMENT

Pre-Wehrmacht equipment

German field equipment used in World War II differed little outwardly from that used in World War I and even earlier, though improved materials and refinements were incorporated alongside the introduction of new items. Between the late 1880s and the late 1900s an infantryman was outfitted with a leather field belt, two large single-compartment cartridge pouches (M1885, M1887, M1989), M1893 bread bag, M1893 field flask (waterbottle), M1893 cook pot (mess tin), small spade and carrier, M1892 shelter quarter, and M1895 pack. The belt, cartridge pouches, and other leather items were normally black, though some were brown. The bread bag (a small haversack) and square tent section/ground cloth were of reddish brown canvas; the latter could be worn as a weather cape, but did not possess a head slit as did the M1931. The M1895 pack was made of the same canvas and its back flap was covered with calfskin (its hair retained for water repellency). This pack had replaced the similar all-canvas M1887. Both packs' shoulder straps had to be attached to the belt in order to carry it.

In the late 1900s much of the equipment was improved. The M1909 three-compartment leather cartridge pouch was adopted to better accommodate the Gew.98 rifle's loading clips. Mounted troops later received the smaller M1911 pouch. An improved M1910 field flask and M1910 cook pot were introduced. The bread bag and tent section began to be made of field grey canvas in 1911, though reddish brown ones continued to be made into World War I. The M1907 pack was constructed of a calfskin (with hair) flap and reddish brown canvas covered wood frame, and included shoulder straps which had to be attached to the belt; in 1913 it was slightly modified (M1907/13). From 1907 leather equipment was generally brown (in conjunction with the introduction of the field grey uniform), though some units were authorised black equipment as part of their uniform distinctions.

This same equipment was used throughout World War I, though the quality of materials deteriorated from 1916. The troops in the trenches soon found that blackened leather equipment provided more effective camouflage, and in September 1915 this practice was officially sanctioned in regulations. Most canvas items were field grey, though reddish brown and other brown and grey shades were used. Gas mask cases were introduced in 1916. Pre-1907 equipment was usually issued to *Reserve* (first-line reserve), *Landwehr* (State Defence—second-line reserve), and *Landsturm* (State Assault—home guard) units.

The post-1918 *Reichswehr* period initially saw the continued use of the above equipment, though now manufactured with upgraded materials to include the expanded use of leather. The M1911 cartridge pouch replaced the M1909 as Army-wide standard in 1933. In early 1934 the M1907/13 pack was again modified (without redesignation) by the addition of an internal canvas pocket for the cook pot for camouflage purposes (it was previously attached to the outside). In the early 1930s a wide variety of new equipment items were introduced. Though generally of similar design to earlier items, they incorporated many refinements and higher quality materials. Both black and brown leather items were used. Canvas items were field grey, olive green, brown, grey, and tan. It was with this equipment that the German soldier entered World War II.

Army field equipment

The basic individual field equipment (*Feldausrüstung des Mannes*) with which German infantry riflemen and other combat troops (*Fechtende Truppen*) were equipped was composed of an integrated system of items designed to complement each other in their wear and practical use. Though specialists were issued a wide variety of unique items, the basic system served as a foundation for all individual equipment. Ammunition pouches for weapons other than carbines (machine pistols, assault rifles, etc.) were issued with the weapon.

The field equipment issued to a rifleman at the outbreak of

Infantry troops conducting assault training early in the war. Though fully laden with equipment, they possess no support straps. (Author's collection)

Pioneer assault troops during an early war training exercise. The long expedient 'bangalore torpedo' is constructed of M1928 200g demolition charges fastened to a plank. (Author's collection)

the war consisted of a leather belt to which two carbine cartridge pouches were attached, to the right and left front. Belt support straps (introduced just prior to the war in conjunction with new packs, tested since 1937) were attached to the belt (at the back) and cartridge pouches at the front, thus making the three components (belt, pouches, support straps) an integrated system (earlier model support straps were still in use). The bread bag was attached to the belt over the right rear. The field flask was attached to the outside of the bread bag. The small entrenching tool and carrier were attached to the belt over the left hip, with the bayonet fastened by its frog to the carrier or belt depending on the model. The gas mask, carried in a cylindrical steel canister, was slung over the left shoulder by a strap, fastened to the belt, and positioned over the bread bag. Several alternative carrying positions were prescribed to accommodate specific duty requirements. A gas sheet, carried in a small pouch, was attached to the mask canister strap over the wearer's chest. When no form of pack was worn, the cook pot was attached to the bread bag beside the field flask, or secured to the belt support straps on the wearer's back. The tent quarter (combination weather cape, ground cloth, tent section) was usually fastened to the support straps below the cook pot. This combination provided the rifleman with a minimum of equipment needed to function effectively in the field for up to 24 hours—a means to carry ammunition, sidearm (bayonet), rations, water, cooking utensils, and small subsistence items. It also provided necessary battlefield survival equipment: gas mask, gas sheet, entrenching tool, and tent quarter.

Additional items could be carried with the aid of the combat pack, introduced just prior to the war. This web pack frame was secured to the back of the support straps and included a small bag for additional subsistence items. The tent quarter and its accessories were attached to the frame along with the cook pot. In order to carry a more substantial existence load, a pack was provided in which to carry additional clothing, weather protection gear (greatcoat and/or blanket), rations, and subsistence and minimal comfort items. The cook pot was placed inside the pack

when it was carried. Pre-war issue packs still had to be attached to the belt by their shoulder straps, but just prior to the war one was adopted which attached directly to the support straps. Equipment carried on the soldier was referred to as march baggage (*Marschegepäck*). Soldiers were also issued a small clothing bag to carry additional clothing; in the field this *Trossgepäck* was carried by a unit's baggage train along with the pack when not carried in combat. Standard contents of the different packs and bags are discussed in a later section of the text.

As can be seen, the entire system was well thought-out allowing a commander to choose a number of levels of individual equipment loads to most effectively accomplish his unit's mission. As the conflict wore on additional items were introduced and a wide variety of carrying positions, official and unofficial, evolved to accommodate the realities of the battlefield.

Tropical equipment

Special equipment items were manufactured for use in North Africa from late 1940 to 1942 to withstand the rigours of a hot, dry climate. Referred to as tropical equipment (*tropisch Ausrüstung*), they were fabricated principally of canvas and webbing in lieu of leather wherever possible. For almost all items of the basic Continental rifleman's equipment there was a tropical counterpart. Most of this was reed green, though sand colour, tan, and light brown were used to lesser degrees. Painted metal components were also usually of these colours. The few leather items and components used were generally tan or light brown. Black and dark brown leather Continental equipment was sometimes painted sand or tan.

Not all troops serving in Africa were issued tropical equipment; by 1942 a large number of units had been rapidly transferred to the theatre along with their Continental equipment. Due to the deteriorating supply situation little tropical equipment was issued after early 1942. Tropical items were also worn mixed with Continental equipment.

Some collectors are quick to assume that almost any item

fabricated of canvas and webbing and of reed green, sand, tan, or light brown coloration is tropical equipment, but this is not always the case. Additionally, from 1943, many metal items were painted dark yellow regardless of issue. The manufacture of canvas/web equipment was increased from 1943, and though generally of various green shades, it was also made in reed green and tan. The purpose of its issue was to conserve leather and provide more durable and lighter weight equipment, and as such it was widely issued to units on the Continent. There were also a number of organisations outside the *Wehrmacht* which utilised military-style equipment in various shades of brown and tan. Collectors are quick to note the scarcity of actual tropical equipment; it appears that huge quantities of captured gear were burned by the Allies after the May 1943 German capitulation in North Africa.

Other services' equipment

The **Waffen-SS** used basically the same equipment as the Army with only a small number of unique items issued. A wide range of special ammunition pouches were utilised by the *Waffen-SS* to

The gun leader of a 150mm sIG33 heavy infantry gun records firing data while wearing equipment typical of infantry gun and artillery gun and artillery crews. Two of these weapons were organic to an infantry regiment's infantry gun company, along with six 75mm infantry guns, and were manned by specially trained infantrymen rather than artillerymen. (Author's collection)

accommodate the many 'odd' models of captured and impounded weapons they used alongside standard issue. Within Germany the *Waffen-SS* maintained its own equipment supply establishments and even conducted limited manufacturing. In the combat zones, since most *Waffen-SS* units fell under Army command, they relied on the senior branch for much of their equipment needs. The *Waffen-SS* also tended to follow the Army's lead in the design, issue, distribution, and allowance of field equipment. Army directives were usually followed by the *Waffen-SS* issuing their own, ordering the same guidelines or compliance. While some leather items were dark brown, black predominated. Canvas and webbing was usually field grey or olive green. Hardware was usually painted field grey or various other shades of grey.

The *Luftwaffe* too maintained its own supply system autonomous of the Army's. Though similar in design to the Army's equipment, that of the *Luftwaffe* was generally made of light brown leather and blue grey (*blaugrau*) canvas/webbing. Most metal items and hardware were also painted blue grey. A number of special canvas/webbing items were issued to the parachute troops, in blue grey, olive green, and 'splinter' camouflage patterns. As the war progressed the parachute troops, now fighting in purely a ground rôle, were issued principally Army equipment. This also applied to the *Luftwaffe* field divisions when transferred to Army control in late 1943.

Some of the various paramilitary, police, and political organisations in the Third Reich issued their own equipment items. Most of these used packs, bread bags, and field flasks similar to the Army's, though colour differences are found; brown and tan leather and canvas predominated. The 'Brownshirts' of the *Sturmabteilung—SA*[1], one of the largest of these paramilitary organisations, and the Political Leadership of the National Socialist German Workers' Party, were issued light brown equipment manufactured especially for these organisations. Some of this was used by the Army on a limited basis late in the war. The Order Police (*Ordnungspolizei*), the normal police, were issued brown leather equipment. Militarised State Police (*Landespolizei*) units were issued both brown and black leather equipment and initially retained it when incorporated into the Army in 1935. Other organisations (Organisation Todt, National Labour Service, National Socialist Motor Corps, Technical Emergency Service, Red Cross, etc.) with support elements serving with the Field Army were often issued Army equipment. All forms of early and late model Army equipment, as well as that of other organisations, were used by the *Volkssturm*.

Only limited use was made of captured and impounded equipment by first-line German armed forces, usually in the form of ammunition pouches and containers to accommodate captured weapons. *Ost Truppen* (Eastern Troops) formations, composed of Soviet defectors, were often issued captured Red Army equipment. This and other equipment, captured or impounded in occupied countries, were also issued to locally raised German-controlled rear area security organisations.

Equipment procurement and issue

The wear, distribution, and modification of equipment was governed by Army Service Instructions (*Heeresdienstvorschriften—HDv*—service manuals) and Army Order Books (*Heeresverordnungsblatten—HV*—general orders). It must be pointed out that when changes in construction, materials, colour,

[1] See MAA 220. *The SA 1921–45: Hitler's Stormtroopers.*

etc., were directed in these orders, it was seldom that existing items were modified; typically they were ordered to be used until worn out.

Unit War Strength Authorisations (*Kriegsstärkenachweis-ungen*—*KStN*), War Equipment Authorisations (*Kriegsaus-rüstungsnachweisungen*—*KAN*), and their Annexes (*Anlagen*) were very specific as to which individuals and types of units were authorised particular equipment items. Allocation changes were made throughout the war in order to provide specialised units and individuals with items of more utility as well as conserve items in critically short supply. Levels of equipment authorisation also varied greatly between the *Feldheer* (Field Army) and the *Ersatzheer* (Replacement Army—administrative command and service organisations; security and replacement units; schools, demonstration and experimental troops). As in World War I *Ersatz Reserve* and *Landsschützen* (State Rifle—security) units were issued older *Reichswehr* equipment, especially early in the war. As the war progressed most of the older equipment was replaced with current designs, but still in reduced allowances. Late in the war, in order to conserve equipment items, 'wear-out' periods were extended as replacements were often simply not available.

Equipment requirements and manufacturing specifications were established by the General Army Office/Staff/Clothing (*Allgemeines Heeresamt*/*Stab*/*Bekleidung*). Procurement of equipment began at the Defence Forces Clothing and Equipment Office (*Wehrmachtbeschaffungsamt Bekleidung und Ausrüstung*) in Berlin with the purchase of raw materials for issue to the various Army Clothing Offices (*Heeresbekleidungsamter*—*HBA*) for manufacture. These depots were also responsible for the forwarding of manufactured goods, their issue, repair of equipment

An assault squad advances across a French field, 1940. The soldier in the rear carries a cluster charge (Geballte Ladung), a stick grenade with six additional grenade heads, *handles removed, lashed around it. The soldier in front of him carries a 7.92mm Pz.B.39 anti-tank rifle. All are outfitted with combat packs. (Author's collection)*

in mass quantities, and disposition of captured equipment. There was at least one HBA established in each defence district, under the control of Section E, Defence District Administration (*Sachgebiet E, Wehrkriesverwaltung*). The HBA itself controlled several organisations. The Testing and Repair Departments (*Verwaltungs und Instandsetzungabteilungen*) repaired damaged equipment. Both Army Clothing Depots (*Heeresbekleidungs-largern*) and Army Clothing Branch Depots (*Heeresbekleidungs-nebenlargern*) processed and issued equipment and clothing to field units.

The Army also relied heavily on large and small privately owned business establishments for the contract manufacture of many equipment items and components, a key principle in the National Socialist German Workers' Party economic concepts. Officers purchased some of their field equipment items (map cases, belts, holsters, etc.), for which they received an allowance.

Equipment repairs in support of field units were effected by Army Clothing Repair Workshops (*Heeresbekleidungs-Instandsetzungs-Werkstätten*). Two special types of depots existed for the issue of equipment: Clothing Processing Posts (*Durchschlesungsstellen*) issued initial issue (*erste Ausstattung*) equipment and clothing to replacements en route to field units. Gas Protection Equipment Depots (*Gasschutzgeräteparken*) stocked special chemical protection equipment and clothing.

BASIC EQUIPMENT

The individual field equipment described in this section was that issued to riflemen and other dismounted combat troops. Components were also used by all other personnel as a foundation for their more specialised equipment. A complete set of rifleman's basic field equipment with contents (ammunition, water, rations), but without a pack, weighed about 9 kilograms, or 20 pounds[1].

Belt

The enlisted man's belt (*Koppel*) was a simple black smooth leather equipment support belt 4.5cm wide. The buckle was attached to a leather tongue on the right end allowing it to be adjusted to fit and the left was fitted with a metal catch. Several variations are found: reed green or tan web tropical model (also issued on the Continent from 1943); black *Press-Stoff* and artificial leather as late war economy versions; black patent leather 4cm wide private purchase walking-out dress versions (the inside lined with various colours of cloth).

The belt was worn with all classes of soldiers' and NCOs' uniforms to include field service, walking-out, and parade. It was also worn with the greatcoat in garrison. In the field the belt served to support equipment.

The standard **belt buckle** (*Koppelschloss*) was adopted in January 1936 to replace the similar *Reichswehr* model. It was made of stamped aluminium and painted field or matt grey. The issue buckle was approximately 6.4cm long and 4.9cm wide. A large number of variants will be encountered with both pebbled and smooth finishes, far too numerous to detail here. These included: field grey steel—pre- and early war mass production; olive green steel—tropical issue; dark grey steel—1944 universal

economy; reddish brown Bakelite—limited economy production; bright aluminium or other polished metals—private purchase walking-out. (The same design buckle was used by the *Kriegsmarine*, in dark blue painted and brass plated models, on a brown belt.)

Belt supports

Commonly referred to as '"Y" straps with "D" rings' by collectors, the **belt supports with auxiliary straps** (*Koppeltraggestell mit Hilfstrageriemen*) were composed of a vertical back strap that hooked to the back centre of the belt. It was fastened to a large leather-padded 'O' ring, as were two front straps which ran over the wearer's shoulders and were hooked to either the cartridge pouch 'D' rings or supplementary loops when pouches were not worn. Smaller auxiliary straps were fastened to the front straps near the underarm level for attachment to hooks on the bottom of the M1939 pack, combat pack frame, and some rucksacks (to prevent side sway and bouncing). All five straps were adjustable by buckles and studs (slide buckles on web versions). On the back shoulders of the two front straps were 'D' rings to which the above packs were attached. Two versions were common: black leather—standard issue; and reed green and olive green webbing—tropical and late war issue.

The belt supports were introduced in April 1939 along with the M1939 pack and combat pack frame, which required the support straps in order to carry them. Some models of wartime rucksacks could also be fitted to the belt supports. Prior to this all packs possessed integral carrying straps which were attached to the belt and ammunition pouches. The pack was not intended to be carried into action (the bread bag was used to carry rations and subsistence items in combat), and when it was discarded the soldier was forced to bear the weight of the belt, with its considerable load of attached equipment, on his hips. The belt supports effectively distributed and supported this load as well as providing a means to carry the new packs. The belt supports with auxiliary straps were initially authorised only for infantrymen in

These members of a cyclist squadron oddly wear most of their equipment reversed from the standard method of carrying. The folding spade and bayonet are on the right side and the bread bag and field flask are over the left hip. The M1938 carrying case for gas mask is carried in the standard position. Their Kar.98k carbines are slung in the manner authorised for cyclists and horse-mounted troops. (Author's collection)

[1] One kilogram (kg) is equal to 2.2 pounds.

rifle companies, and in April 1940 were redesignated **belt supports for infantry** (*Koppeltraggestell für Infanterie*). They were authorised for motorcycle rifle and bicycle units in June 1941 and March 1943 respectively. They were also issued with the *Wien 41* mine detector to carry its electronics pack. In the rear areas it was common for the front straps to be worn under the tunic shoulder straps, but this was seldom done under combat conditions. Other types of belt supports were authorised in other units, and are discussed later.

A simpler model, designated **support straps for cartridge pouches**, was issued to support the cartridge pouches and belt prior to 1935, though they continued to be worn, and are described under 'Troop Leaders' Equipment'. They were also issued to non-infantry combat units. They were replaced in late 1934 by modifying the enlisted field tunic with the inclusion of two integral, internal grey web support straps attached to four removable wire side hooks passing through holes at the waist in order to support the belt and attached equipment. This system was ordered removed from infantrymen's tunics in April 1939, and later from cyclists' when they were authorised belt supports. To conserve materials it was ordered not to include the straps and hooks in any tunics made after April 1943.

Supplementary loops
Usually called 'belt loops' or 'belt "D" rings' by collectors, the **supplementary loops** (*Aufschiebeschlaufen*) were constructed of a simple belt-width loop fitted with a 'D' or rectangular ring. They were made of black or brown leather or various colours of webbing. Their original purpose was to provide an attachment point for the front straps of belt supports when ammunition pouches were not worn. They were also used to attach the belt support back strap if it was too short for a tall individual; to attach the field flask to the belt when a bread bag was not worn (turned ring-down); and for other equipment securing purposes.

Cartridge pouches
The standard shoulder weapon was the Kar.98k carbine adopted in 1934, though other models of 7.92mm Mauser rifles and carbines were issued. Their ammunition was carried in the **M1911 cartridge pouch** (*Patronentasche 11*), retained without noticeable change since its adoption. They were constructed of black pebbled leather (smooth will be encountered) with three pockets, sometimes with a pocket divider, fastened to a slightly curved leather backing. The pocket lids were secured by a strap that fastened to a stud on the bottom of each pocket. On the back were two leather belt loops and a 'D' or rectangular ring for attachment to the support straps. Each pocket held two five-round loading clips of 7.92mm ammunition for a total of 30 rounds per pouch. They are often referred to as **M1909 cartridge pouches** by collectors, but this is incorrect. The M1909 was similar, but each pocket held three loading clips for a total of 45 rounds per pouch; they were used by dismounted troops until 1933. The M1911 pouch was originally adopted for mounted troops' use and replaced the M1909 as Army-wide standard in 1933. A very limited number of natural light tan leather pouches were issued for use in North Africa. It must be remembered that other organisations used brown pouches, e.g. the *Luftwaffe* and Order Police. The Polish Army used brown pouches of virtually identical design, which were re-issued by the Germans.

Soldiers in combat units were issued two pouches while those in support and rear service units and the Replacement Army

Soldiers in France clear wreckage from a village alley. All wear the bread bag, gas mask case, bayonet, field flask, and cook pot without benefit of belt support straps. (Author's collection)

received only one. When one was worn (the side it was worn on depended on other equipment) a supplementary loop was required to attach the opposite side belt support strap, if issued.

Bread bag
The bread bag was as much a traditional part of the German uniform as jackboots, having been in use since the early 1800s; earlier models were slightly larger. It was referred to as a 'bread bag' as bread had long been a staple field ration; it is high in calories and filling. The **M1931 bread bag** (*Brotbeutel 31*) was a simple canvas single-compartment haversack. (Some references list an M1934 bread bag, but the M1931 was the only model.) Its flap covered the entire outside of the bag for additional weather protection. At the top corners were buttoned cloth loops to fasten it to the belt. In the top centre was a single cloth support tab fastened to the belt by a hook. At the base of the corner loops were 'D' rings secured by leather tabs, for the attachment of the field flask and cook pot. About two-thirds of the flap's length below the 'D' rings were two leather loops to secure those items' straps and prevent bouncing.

On the bread bag's back surface, behind the corner loops, were small 'D' rings for a shoulder strap; this adjustable cloth strap was fitted with carbine hooks at both ends. It was seldom that the bread bag was carried in this manner, except by some officers, and the straps were usually used for other purposes or

discarded; it and its 'D' rings were deleted from bags made after 1942/43. Two small leather straps were sewn to the inside of the flap corresponding with the outside securing tabs. These were fastened to buttons near the bag's front lower corners, beneath the flap, to further secure the contents. A longer leather strap was sewn to the inside of the bag's back surface, and fastened to a button on the bag's front top edge.

Early bags were field grey. In 1941/42 they began to be produced in olive green. Late in the war they were also made in various shades of grey, brown and tan. An all-canvas reed green tropical bread bag was developed with webbing replacing the leather components.

In November 1944 it was directed that standard issue bread bags be modified both to conserve materials and to introduce a refinement: the belt loops were to be simple sewn cloth loops without buttons, and the centre hooked support tab was also replaced by a loop. This arrangement required that the bag be slipped on to the belt. The leather equipment tabs on the flap were now made of webbing. The refinement was a small strap-and-button secured pocket on the bag's right front under the flap, to take the carbine cleaning kit.

A wide variety of non-military bread bags were utilised by the many political and para-military organisations, similar to the Army's and were often in various shades of brown and tan. That used by the *Sturmabteilung* was sometimes retained when selected SA units were incorporated into the Army, as well as being issued late in the war as a substitute. These light brown bags differed from the Army's in having a 'D' ring only on the left corner, no securing loops on the flap, an internal divider with two integral pockets, and brown leather flap edge binding.

The bread bag was worn over the right hip, often with the field flask attached to a corner 'D' ring, and sometimes the cook pot as well. The bag's contents might include (not all of the following items could be carried at once) an iron ration, eating utensils[1], meat container (*Fleischbüchse*), fat box (*Fettdose* — fat or butter for cooking), small folding field stove (*Esbit Kocher*), hexamethylene tetramine fuel tablets (*Esbit Brennstoff*), M1934 carbine cleaning kit (*Reinigungsgerät 34*)[2], washing kit (*Waschzeug*), shaving kit (*Rasierzeug*), sewing kit (*Nähzeug*), and field cap when not being worn. The personal kits were usually contained in small drawstring oilskin or fabric bags.

Field flask

Though a standard design was common, there were perhaps more distinct variants of this item found than with any other piece of equipment. The standard **M1931 field flask and drinking cup** (*Feldflasche 31 und Trinkbecker*) was an unpainted aluminium .8 litre (approximately 28 ounce) bottle; earlier models had no cup. A metal screw cap was retained by an extension of the vertical leather securing strap. A brown felt insulating cover was provided, both to prevent freezing and to cool the water when wet; it was removable, for cleaning or replacement, by the incorporation of a slit secured by three snaps on the left upper edge. Leather loops were sewn on the front and back for the black leather securing strap, also attached by a stud riveted to the bottom of the cover. The securing strap served to retain the cup, and to attach the canteen to the bread bag or

---

[1] Common eating utensils included the *Essbesteck* interlocking set with knife, fork, spoon and can opener; M1910 combined folding fork and spoon; normal mess hall issue knife, fork and spoon; or 'liberated' tableware.

[2] The carbine cleaning kit consisted of a chain 'pull through', two bore brushes, oil can, and disassembly tool contained in a grey metal can.

Lightly equipped troops practise beach defence on the French coast early in the war. They wear their white denim work trousers to prevent wear and tear of their wool trousers. The MG34 heavy machine gunner appears, oddly, to have a Mauser C96 'broomhandle' pistol shoulder stock/holster on his hip, possibly indicating a second-line static defence unit. (Author's collection)

Early war M1931 bread bags. Both are olive green with black leather fittings. (Troy Haley collection)

elsewhere by a carbine hook attached to it. The strap was fitted with a buckle to adjust fit. In North Africa two canteens were sometimes issued.

The oval-shaped drinking cup was made of aluminium and originally painted black, though ordered painted olive green in April 1941. A bracket was riveted to one side through which the securing strap passed. On the other side was a two-piece folding wire handle, held in place by the securing strap. The cup was stored upside down with the handle toward the body.

Variants were many. Late war field flasks were made of painted and unpainted steel, and different coloured felts were used including greens and greys. Enamelled steel bottles were also made, as well as bottles covered with a dark brown or brown speckled phenolic resin composition (serving only to prevent freezing) with a cap of the same material. Web side loops and securing straps, with slide buckles, were fitted to tropical covers and on many late war versions, including those with the composition covering. This flask possessed an additional web strap around the circumference. Bakelite screw caps were also used; and small round black Bakelite and steel cups were issued. A large number of similar non-military versions were also manufactured.

Cook pot

The traditional German cook pot (mess kit) was copied by many European countries, and these are sometimes misidentified as German. The kidney-shaped cross-section **M1931 cook pot** (*Kochgeschirr 31*) was composed of two components, the pan and pot. The shallow pan could be used for eating or cooking, and served as a lid for the pot; it was fitted with a folding steel handle that also held it to the pot when stowed. The 1.7 litre (about 57 ounce) pot was fitted with a wire bail handle, and used for eating soups and stews. Earlier models were somewhat larger, 2.5 litre (about 85 ounce), and painted field grey. The M1931 cook pot was made of aluminium until about 1943 when most began to be made of steel. A metal bracket was fitted to the pan's handle

through which a black leather securing strap was passed, holding the two sections together and securing it for carrying. The outer surfaces were painted dark grey until April 1941, when it was ordered that new cook pots be olive green. A limited number of reed green painted cook pots with reed green web securing straps were issued for use in North Africa.

The cook pot was carried attached to the outside of earlier model packs and rucksacks and inside later models, strapped to the bread bag beside the canteen, or secured to the combat pack frame or the back of the support straps. Preserved bread or other rations were often carried inside.

Entrenching tools

Several different models of spades (*Spaten*) were used. Some captured models were issued as well, especially the Polish equivalent, which was similar to the German small entrenching tool but with a bluntly pointed blade. The entrenching tool and carrier were worn on the left side of the belt.

The **small entrenching tool** (*kleines Schanzzeug*) was a simple spade with a square steel blade and short wood handle, basically unchanged since the 1880s and similar to that used by most European armies. Its blade was painted black (sometimes tan or sand colour in North Africa) and the handle was unpainted, to prevent the hands from blistering, though they were varnished when manufactured. Its overall length was just over 50cm, though this varied.

The **carrier for small entrenching tool** (*Tasche für kleines Schanzzeug*) was composed of a blade-shaped leather back panel with a leather rim on the front (referred to as 'closed-back' by collectors). Fastened to the top were two leather belt loops. A leather securing strap was fitted to the right side of the rim and the buckled end to the left; the tool was inserted into the carrier and the securing strap wrapped around its handle where it joined the blade. Variants were made without a solid back panel, but with a rim similar to that on the front (called 'open-backed' or 'skeletonised' by collectors). Prior to the mid-1930s carriers were

A mountain artillery troop with its Czech-made 150mm L15 mountain cannon. Seven horses/mules were required to pack this impounded weapon. (Author's collection)

dark brown, but most later ones were black. From April 1938 most carriers were made of black artificial leather; the belt loops and securing strap were still required to be of real leather, and this also applied to the carriers for the later folding entrenching tools. Late war carriers were made of black or light tan *Press-Stoff* but still with real leather loops and straps. Limited issue was made of a reed green canvas and web model, of the same basic design as the 'closed-back' version, in North Africa. The bayonet frog was positioned on the belt between the carrier's two belt loops and the tool's retaining strap wrapped around the scabbard as well as the tool's handle. This was not invariably done in the field, and the bayonet was often carried on the belt just forward of the entrenching tool carrier.

The Austrian **spade for infantry** (*Spaten für Infanterie*) was used by former Austrian Federal Army units inducted into the German Army in 1938. It was similar to the above German model, but had a bluntly pointed blade. The light brown leather carrier had a single narrow buckled leather belt loop fitted on the carrier's point by a 'D' ring, but was otherwise similar to the German model, and is found in both solid-back and open-back versions.

The **folding spade** (*Klappspaten*) was an innovative design introduced in November 1938, though it did not come into common usage until after the outbreak of war. Its purpose was to

provide the infantryman with a more substantial shovel, that is a longer handle, without increasing the overall carrying length; it also allowed the tool to be used as a substitute for the pick, with the pointed blade locked in a 90-degree position. Its unfolded length was about 70cm, 50cm folded. The blade was black-painted (tan or sand colour in North Africa) steel, with a locking nut made of phenolic resin cast with a steel ring. This tool was copied by the US Army in 1943.

Early **carriers for folding spade** (*Tasche für Klappspaten*) were of black artificial or real leather, but later ones were of light tan *Press-Stoff* with a solid back panel and a real leather outer rim. The tool was slipped into the top and held in place by a wide leather strap fastened to a stud affixed to a thin cross-strap. The blade's tip fitted into a leather pocket housing a metal protector. The later wartime version had a solid back panel, but leather retaining side strips were fitted rather than a full rim; the bottom was open. A narrow retaining flap was fitted across the top to which a thin securing strap was attached; this fastened to a thin cross-strap attached to the edge strips. Both types had a wide leather belt loop riveted to the back panel. A bayonet scabbard retaining loop was riveted to the lower left back panel; the bayonet frog itself was worn on the belt forward of the carrier. A canvas/web model is not known, but should not be ruled out.

Sidearm carriers

The **sidearm carrier** (*Seitengewehrtasche*), or bayonet frog, was designed to carry the steel scabbard (*Scheide*) of the bayonet (*Bajonett*, or more commonly, *Seitengewehr*—sidearm) attached to the belt; German scabbards did not possess an integral belt attachment, so a frog was required for this purpose. Scabbards had a lug fitted to the upper outside surface which held it in the frog. The bayonet was worn on the left hip. If the entrenching tool was carried, it was worn in conjunction with it (see above). Though designed for the standard Kar.98k carbine's S.84/98 bayonet (adopted as standard for the Kar.98k in 1934, variants bearing this designation being issued since 1900), all other German and some captured models could be fitted to the listed frogs. All models were similarly constructed, with a backing which also doubled as the belt loop, a scabbard retaining band with a lug eyelet, and a stud-secured hilt retaining strap on most. Several versions were produced:

Sidearm frog for dismounted troops (*Seitengewehrtasche für Unberittene*)—black leather with a tapered backing and without retaining straps.

Sidearm frog for mounted troops (*Seitengewehrtasche für Berittene*)—black leather with a tapered backing, but with retaining straps. In January 1939 it was ordered that this model be issued to all troops to reduce the loss of bayonets. The dismounted model was to have the retaining straps added, though this was often not accomplished.

Sidearm frog for tropical use (*Seitengewehrtasche für tropisch*)—reed green webbing with straight backing and retaining strap. This model was also issued late in the war, often in different colours, and sometimes without the retaining straps.

Late war issue—black leather with narrow straight backing and leather retaining straps. These were also made with various coloured web backings and the other components of leather. Limited issue from late 1942.

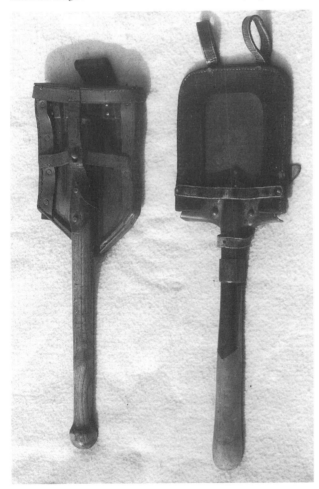

Left: A folding spade with the early model carrier; painted field grey. Right: A small entrenching tool with a 'closed-back' carrier. (Troy Haley collection)

Private purchase—patent leather of a design similar to the dismounted model, but without retaining straps, worn with the walking-out uniform. The backs were sometimes lined with coloured cloth.

Officer's model—during the Third Reich period few officers wore bayonets, though this had earlier been a common practice. It was very similar to the enlisted man's black dismounted model, but was light reddish brown (orange colour) with a thin pressed line or groove around the edges. This should not be mistaken for an enlisted man's or tropical variant.

Sidearm knots—for dismounted troops, tassels (*Troddeln*), and for mounted troops, hand straps (*Faustriemen*)—were worn in garrison and on parade attached to the frog. They were even sometimes worn in the field, but this practice was discontinued early in the war. These multicoloured knots served to identify companies/squadrons/batteries within a regiment or separate battalion.

Gas mask cases

Three models of **gas masks** were used by the Germans: the *Gasmaske 24, 30, und 38*. The M1924 mask was fitted with a hose attached to an oval-shaped filter. Field troops carried it in an elongated grey canvas case slung over the shoulder and carried at the left hip. Its filter was encased in brown leather when used with this case. Rear area troops used a field grey canvas and brown leather haversack-type case, also carried by a shoulder strap. During the war the M1924 mask and these cases were used only by Replacement Army personnel and saw only limited use.

The M1930 and M1938 masks were of similar design, but the M1930 was made of rubberised cloth and leather while the M1938 was entirely of rubber. Both of these masks used a round filter canister attached to the snout of the face piece. Several types of field grey painted filters were issued including special dust-resistant tropical models. Individuals requiring corrective lenses were issued special mask spectacles (*Maskenbrille*) that could be fitted inside the mask.

Three models of **carrying case for gas mask** (*Tragbüchse für Gasmaske*) were issued and were interchangeable between the M1930 and M1938 masks. They consisted of a robust, rather heavy fluted steel canister with a hinged lid. Inside the lid was a hinged compartment for spare eyepiece lenses. The lid was held closed by a spring-loaded latch fitted with a web pull strap. Below the lid, on the right side in relation to the latch, were two small brackets to which an adjustable web carrying sling was fastened. In line with these, at the canister's bottom edge, was a third bracket with a short web support tab and belt hook. The M1930 case was 24.5cm long, 12cm in diameter, and easily identifiable by its deep lid. It was replaced by the M1938 case, but still used in training and second-line units. The M1938 case was 24.5cm long, 12.5cm in diameter, and had a shallow lid. In November 1941 it was ordered that new cases be made 2.5cm longer to better accommodate the mask, 12cm in diameter, and fitted with an improved latch. In April 1942 it was ordered that the shorter cases be issued to the Replacement Army, replacing the M1930

case, and the lengthened models given only to the Field Army. Issued in field grey, it was not unusual for them to be painted different colours in the field; various shades of green, brown, and tan (especially in North Africa, along with sand colour). They were sometimes painted white or whitewashed in the winter.

Each man carried a small brown plastic box containing ten losantine tablets (*Losantintabletten*) used for skin decontamination of blister agents. These were later replaced by skin decontamination salve (*Hautentgiftungsalbe 41*), issued in a brown plastic bottle carried in a dark orange-brown cardboard box along with six cotton swabs. These items were carried in the mask case.

The normal method of wear for infantrymen prescribed that the case be positioned over the bread bag (worn on the right rear) just below the belt, with the lid to the wearer's right for easy access, though it was common for it to be worn with the lid to the left. The sling was worn over the left shoulder and adjusted to maintain the case in an almost horizontal position. The short support tab near the bottom end was hooked to the belt between the bread bag's left loop and centre support tab. There were a wide variety of other prescribed carrying positions depending on the wearer's duties:

Machine gunners—worn in the same manner as riflemen's, but reversed with the lid to the left side. (Also carried in this manner

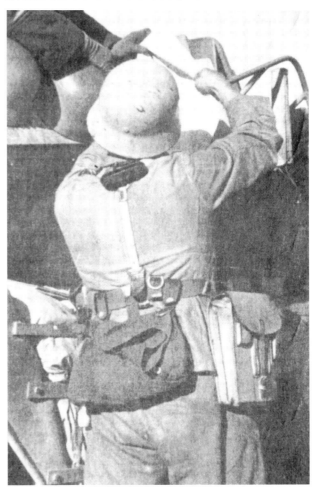

An officer in North Africa is outfitted with a tropical web belt, Continental issue bread bag, tan-painted M1935 report/map case, and tan-painted 'belt supports for officers' (had been designated 'support straps for cartridge pouches' prior to April 1940). His binoculars' eyepiece protector has worked its way behind his neck. (US Army)

by others whose special equipment would interfere with the case in the normal position.)

Drivers and motorcyclists—worn horizontally on the chest with the shortened sling around the neck and the lid to the right.

Mounted troops—worn on the right hip below the belt and with the sling under the belt to prevent bouncing.

Vehicle passengers—the belt support tab was unfastened and the case moved around to the front and held in the lap, allowing the wearer to rest against the seat.

Mountain troops—attached horizontally to the back of the rucksack, lid to the right, to prevent it interfering with climbing. It would be worn normally if the rucksack was not carried.

In practice they were often worn in whatever manner the wearer found the least encumbering.

Gas sheet

The **gas sheet** (*Gasplane*) was a treated protective fabric or paper sheet intended to protect an individual from sprayed blister agents, such as mustard gas. The 2×1.2 metre gas sheet was made of a wide variety of materials in various colours, including: dark bluish green (original issue), grey, black, and tan rubberised fabrics, the last for tropical use; field grey, grey, brown, and tan viscose-treated fabrics; black, dark blue, and dark and light brown nylon, the last two for tropical use; grey and tan opanol-treated (synthetic rubber) heavy paper, the last for tropical use; light green and black waxed crepe or other papers, a late war economy measure. Most of those intended for tropical use were marked 'TP' or 'tp'.

The gas sheet was originally carried in a small dark bluish green (*blaulich-dunkelgrün*) rubberised fabric pouch. Tropical pouches were of the same material, but tan. From 1942/43 they were also made in field grey and olive green untreated linen. The pouch's flap was secured by two small snaps, each with a pull-tab; on the back were two small fabric loops. The pouch was worn on the gas mask case sling, over the chest, secured by the loops on the back. This manner of wear caused it to bounce around somewhat and it was often reversed and worn between the sling and chest. A more popular method was to secure it to the gas mask case with rubber bands or small leather or web straps. Numerous orders, often ignored, were issued prohibiting this practice, as the pressure of the rubber bands and straps eventually damaged the sheet. In December 1942 a method was approved by which the gas sheet could be secured to the mask case: the sling's free end was extended through its upper bracket and fastened to the belt support tab's bracket. This provided a strap running the length of the case to which the gas sheet pouch could be attached by its back loops.

Members of 5th Sqn., 27th Recon. Bn., clad in motorcycle protective suits, manhandle a motorcycle across a Russian ditch, 1941. The carbine and gas mask case are slung as prescribed for motorcyclists.

Interestingly the M1926 cavalry saddle bags are attached to the machine's rear rather than the usual much larger motorcycle saddle bags (Packtasche für Kradrad). (Author's collection)

Packs

The **M1934 pack** (*Tornister 34*) adopted in November 1934 was similar to earlier models. It was constructed of olive green, brown, tan, or reed green canvas. The leather edge binding and small straps were brown while the shoulder straps were black, though there were variations. The back flap was covered with unshaven calfskin. From the late 1930s some packs were made without the calfskin, having only a canvas back flap; this does not represent a different model. To the inside of the flap was sewn a large pocket, secured by either a small strap and buckle or button. The main compartment was further closed by two flaps secured by two or three leather straps and buckles. Inside the main compartment's upper portion was sewn a cook pot pocket. The flap was secured by two leather straps that attached to buckles on the pack's bottom surface, which also bore a leather tab that hooked to the back centre of the waist belt. Wide adjustable shoulder straps at the top corners were fastened by rivets to leather-covered metal plates. To these were attached small auxiliary straps that fastened to 'D' rings on the pack's bottom. Three pairs of leather loops were fitted to the lower sides and top centre, to which the greatcoat roll was attached (see below).

The **M1939 pack** (*Tornister 39*) was introduced in April 1939 in conjunction with the support straps, which were required to carry the pack. The pack itself was of almost identical design to the M1934. Instead of integral shoulder straps, two large 'D' rings with hooks were fitted in their place at the top. These fastened to the 'D' rings on the back shoulders of the belt support straps. The auxiliary support straps attached with hooks to two more 'D' rings fitted to the pack's bottom. Like the M1934, the M1939 will be found with both calfskin-covered and canvas back flaps.

Prescribed contents were the same for these infantryman's packs. In the main compartment were: laced top shoes placed on either side (left, with polish and cloth inside; right, with shoe brushes inside); cook pot in its pocket (preserved bread inside); tent accessory pouch (see below for contents); carbine cleaning kit, rolled in breech cover, one pair of wool socks; sweater (in autumn and winter); and one iron ration meat tin.

Inside the back flap were: shaving kit, washing kit, sewing kit, towel, handkerchiefs, and undershirt. Under wartime field conditions the contents were often changed to meet specific requirements, but generally remained similar to the above.

Cyclist units, when mounted, carried their packs on a rack behind the seat. In late 1941 various patterns of battle rucksacks were issued to many infantry units in lieu of a standard pack; this was especially the case on the East Front and North Africa. These are described in the 'Specialised Equipment' section under mountain troops.

Combat pack

An innovative light pack system, the **combat pack for infantry rifle companies** (*Gefechtsgepäck für Infanterie Schützenkompanien*) was adopted in April 1939 along with the support straps and M1939 pack (and often called the 'battle' or 'assault pack' by collectors). As the name implies, it was initially issued only to infantrymen in rifle companies, and in the war's early days was in short supply. The principal component was an olive green semi-rigid trapezoid-shaped web pack frame (*Gurtbandtragegerüst*)— referred to as an 'A' frame by collectors. 'D' rings with hooks were fixed to each of its four corners, the upper pair for attachment to the support strap 'D' rings mounted behind the shoulders. The support straps' auxiliary straps were attached to

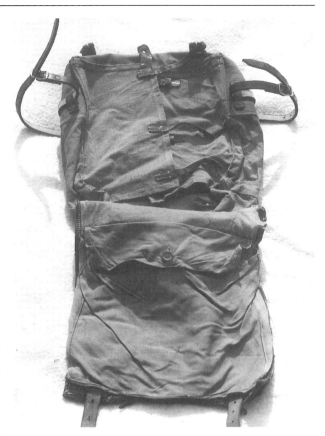

The interior of an M1934 pack. The interior of an M1939 pack was almost identical (Troy Haley collection)

the lower pair. On the lower portion of the frame were two buckle-secured web straps to hold the tent quarter. Two small rectangular rings were fitted to the lower edges to attach the bag (below).

The second component was the **bag for the combat pack** (*Beutel zum Gefechtsgepäck*)—called an 'A' frame bag by collectors. This small olive or reed green bag (later versions were of grey and brown shades) was closed by a flap secured by two tie-tapes through small grommets at its corners. Inside the flap was a small pocket for the carbine cleaning kit. A narrow leather strap was attached inside the flap and further secured the bag's contents by fastening to a button on the outside. The bag was attached to the pack frame by two small web tabs fitted with a button and hole, these passing through the rectangular rings on the pack frame's lower edges.

The bag was small, and served only to redistribute some items from the bread bag, e.g.: undershirt, carbine cleaning kit, eating utensils, fat container, *Esbit* stove, one emergency iron ration meat tin, and tent quarter rope. The cook pot was usually strapped to the upper portion of the frame, sideways, above the tent quarter and bag. Occasionally the tent accessory pouch was strapped to the assembly.

A platoon digs in in a Russian field, 1941. To the right, personnel treat a wounded soldier. A unit medical orderly, with the Geneva Convention arm band, is equipped with the dismounted medical pouches, one of which can be seen under his arm band. The other medic is a fully qualified medical sergeant, designated by the cuff badge, and has a larger unidentified type of medical kit. The two riflemen to the left have full equipment including the combat pack. (Author's collection)

Tent quarter

The **M1931 tent quarter** (*Zeltbahn 31*) replaced an earlier grey square model and was originally known as the '*Warei*' pattern. It was a triangular, water-repellent, cotton gabardine twill multi-purpose shelter, ground cloth, and rain cape. On one side was printed a dark camouflage pattern (*dunklerer Buntfarbenaufdrud*) and on the other a light pattern (*hellerer B.*); these are known to collectors as the three-colour (brown and two shades of green) 'splinter' pattern. Many late war production tent quarters were printed with the dark pattern on both sides. A limited number of reed green or light tan (both sides) models were issued for use in North Africa, but the Continental version was widely used there. Two sides were 203cm (about 6 ft. 7 in.) long, and the base 250cm (about 8 ft. 2 in.). On the short edges were 12 buttonholes and buttons. On the base edge were six small grommets, through which a drawstring was passed, and buttonholes; well above the buttonholes were six buttons. The buttons and holes on the short edges were for attaching together additional tent quarters to construct various sized tents. The buttons and holes at the base were for fastening the tent quarter around the wearer's legs when used as a rain cape. In the centre was a slit, closed by two overlapping flaps, for the wearer's head; when originally adopted a pointed detachable hood was issued, but this was soon deleted. In each corner was a large grommet for tent stakes or rope, as required by the form of tent constructed.

As a tent, one or two tent quarters could be rigged as a simple 'fly' shelter; four could be fastened together for a four-man pyramid tent. There were also standard designs for eight- and 16-man tents. A set of **tent equipment** (*Zeltausrüstung*) was provided for this purpose: a black two-metre tent rope (*Zeltleine*), a four-section (37cm each) wooden tent pole (*Zeltstod*), and two tent stakes (*Zeltpflöde*), all carried in a tent accessories pouch (*Zeltzubehörtasche*). The gabardine or light canvas pouch was grey, camouflage, field grey, olive green, reed green (tropical), brown, or tan, and closed by a one- or two-button flap. Early examples had two leather straps on one edge for securing to other equipment; others had two leather securing loops, or no means of attachment. The tent pins were made of light alloy, steel, or phenolic resin-treated wood. All had an eyelet with a looped cord to aid in extraction.

When the tent quarter was worn as a rain cape (*Regenmantel*) three manners of wear were prescribed to provide maximum protection and freedom of movement: dismounted, mounted, and bicycle. It was also used as a ground sheet or bedroll; and one or two could be rigged as an expedient flotation device when filled with cut limbs or straw and rolled into a bundle.

It could be carried by attaching it to the support straps, combat pack, or back of the belt; rolled into a 'horseshoe roll' (with or without the greatcoat and/or blanket—see below) and fastened to the pack; or carried inside the pack or rucksack. There was a severe shortage of replacement tent quarters in 1944 and issue was limited to selected field units. Limited use was made of captured equivalent shelter quarters and capes, especially square light olive drab Soviet models, with or without hoods.

Greatcoat roll

The **greatcoat roll** (*Mantelrolle*) was a 'horseshoe roll' made up of the blanket and tent quarter in summer months, the greatcoat being added in the autumn and winter. The roll was attached to the pack by three **greatcoat straps for foot troops** (*Mantelriemen für Fusstruppen*). These black leather straps were about 52cm long and secured by buckles. A buttoning strap was fitted to the main strap that served to attach the strap to the loops on the pack's sides and top. They were also used for other general equipment securing purposes. A tropical model was made of reed green or tan webbing and later issued Army-wide. Cyclists, when mounted, carried their greatcoat rolls strapped to the bicycle's frame forward of the seat. The standard wool **enlisted man's blanket** (*Mannschaftsdecke*) was dark grey with two wide and six thin light grey stripes at the ends. Late war blankets were grey and brownish grey with different strip colours and patterns, and made of low quality mixed shoddy wool and rayon. After the winter of 1941/42 it was ordered that troops on the Eastern Front be issued two blankets during the winter months—hardly an over-generous allowance, since the German Army did not issue sleeping bags except in the extreme north (Lappland, Arctic Russia); the combination of greatcoat and blanket was considered sufficient.

Clothing bag

Each man in a combat unit issued with a pack received a single **M1931 clothing bag** (*Bekleidungssack 31*), while those in rear area units, and not issued a pack, received two. Originally they were field grey canvas, but from 1941/42 they were generally made in olive green. This item was a simple single-compartment satchel-like bag closed by a flap secured by two buckled leather straps. A leather carrying handle was fitted to the top edge. Leather components could be black or brown. For the infantryman the usual contents included spare clothing items needed only on a limited basis in the field: drill uniform, underwear, socks, tunic collar liner, etc.

Wound packets

Each soldier carried two different size **wound packets** (*Verbandpäckchen*) in a pocket inside the tunic's lower right skirt corner. They were generally of grey cloth wrapped and secured by string. Unfolded, the small model measured about 5 × 8.5cm and the large was 7 × 11cm, both about 2cm thick.

Field rations

Though not an equipment item, field rations are included here since they were a standard content of the various packs and bags. German field rations, or more accurately, portions (*Feldportionen*—field rations; *Feldrationen* were for animals) were rather Spartan when compared to US and British equivalents. These were supplemented by local purchase, foraging, confiscation, and parcels from home (except on the Eastern Front where these latter were restricted; every bit of transport space was needed for combat necessities, which resulted in a flourishing black market). Portions were divided into four categories; the only one relevant here is the 'provisions I' (*Verpflegungssatz I*)

This 75mm lIG18 light infantry gun loader is wearing a canvas and leather M1924 carrying case for gas mask and leather hauling sling during a pre-war exercise. (Author's collection)

issued to troops in the combat zone. It was composed of fresh, dried, tinned, and other preserved foods prepared by unit field kitchens, often in the form of stews and soups, heavily supplemented by bread and potatoes. In North Africa, in order to prevent spoilage, the bread was replaced by *Zwieback* and the potatoes by dried beans; cooking fat/butter was replaced by tinned olive oil, and heavy use made of Italian tinned meat. Several special field provisions were also issued elsewhere.

The most common was the 'march provision' (*Marschverpflegung*) issued to units for distribution to the troops while in transit (foot, truck, rail), and intended to be eaten cold with no special preparation required. However, squads, vehicle crews, etc., often pooled their portions along with other food they acquired and prepared it collectively. It was usually distributed by unit mess personnel to the troops either on a daily or by-meal basis. It was composed of bread, cold meat and sausage and/or cheese, bread spreads (marmalade or 'artificial honey'), substitute coffee or tea, sugar, and cigarettes. No special packaging was used; the components were either tinned, in packets, wrapped in paper, or carried in the meat container, though a field issue preserved black bread was packed in cardboard cartons.

The 'iron portion' (*Eiserne Portion*) was a packaged emergency ration permitted to be consumed only on the order of the unit commander, though it often proved to be the main subsistence under combat conditions. Troops could be issued a full or half portion. This ration was analogous to US C rations. Most items were issued in tins, the coffee and sugar in paper packets, all packaged in a paper bag weighing 825 grammes (about 30 ounces) with packaging: *Zwieback* (hard, thin, 'twice-baked' biscuits)—250g (9 oz.); potted meat (*Fleischkonserve*)—200g (7 oz.); preserved vegetables (*Gemüse*)—150g (5 oz.); substitute coffee (*Kaffee-Ersatz*)—25g (.9 oz.); and salt (*Salz*)—25g (.9 oz.).

A 'half iron portion' (*Halbeiserne Portion*) was composed of only the *Zwieback* and a tin of potted meat. The iron portion was sometimes supplemented with preserved bread or biscuits. A small linen *Zwieback* bag (*Zwiebackbeutel*) was used to carry biscuit or preserved bread inside the pack, bread bag, rucksack, or saddle bag.

Two special compact portions were introduced in 1943-44 for limited issue to troops engaged in direct combat. Similar to US K rations, the large combat packet (*Grosskampfpäcken*) and close combat packet (*Nahkampfpäcken*) were packaged in small cardboard cartons. They were composed of *Zwieback* or other biscuits, chocolate and fruit bars, candy, and cigarettes.

WEAPONS-RELATED EQUIPMENT

Ammunition pouches, other than those for the Kar.98k carbine and its substitutes, were issued with the weapon. Other equipment items under this category, e.g. pistol holsters, grenade bags, and pouches and carriers for weapon accessories, were also usually issued with the weapon.

MP38/MP40 magazine pouches

The MP38 and MP40 9mm machine pistols, commonly known as the 'Schmeisser', were widely issued to squad and platoon leaders as well as some other NCOs and officers in rifle companies and reconnaissance units. They would of course be found in the hands of some enlisted men and within other types of combat units.

The **machine pistol magazine pouches** (*Maschinenpistole-Magazintaschen*) were issued in matched pairs. There were two wartime versions, both made of canvas and similar in design, with three pockets, each holding one 32-round magazine (MP28/II magazines and those of some other machine pistols would also fit). Each pocket was closed by a stud-secured strap, its end retained by a loop. On the lower outside edge of the left pouch was a small pocket for the magazine loading tool. On the back were two angled belt loops; when worn on the belt the pouch tops angled inward to the wearer's middle, though it was not uncommon for them to be mistakenly worn reversed. Fitted on each pouch, at or near the outer upper corners, was a 'D' ring to attach to the belt support straps. The more common olive green and light tan (late war) canvas model had leather flap straps and retaining belt, and support strap loops; some had leather flaps as well. All leather components were black. The short belt support loops protruded at 90 degrees from the outer sides.

Another version was made with the leather components entirely replaced by webbing; originally designed for tropical use, they were also issued elsewhere. The support strap 'D' rings were fitted at the upper outer corner. These are found in reed green and olive green. A black all-leather model saw very limited pre-war issue; it was similar in construction to the first model described above, but with the stud-closed magazine loading tool pocket on the front of the left pouch. Due to wartime shortages it was not uncommon for only one to be carried, or even for magazines to be carried in tunic skirt pockets. (This applied to other weapons' magazines and pouches as well.)

Gew.43 rifle magazine pouches

The Gew.43 semi-automatic rifle (a slightly shorter carbine version, the Kar.43, saw limited issue) used a ten-round detachable magazine. These weapons were of limited issue, beginning in 1944, usually with only one being issued to a rifle squad in the units that did receive it.

A late war clothing bag, olive green with brown leather fittings. (Troy Haley collection)

The two-pocket **self-loading weapon magazine pouches** (*Selbstladewaffe-Magazintaschen*), each pocket holding one magazine, was issued along with three magazines (one in the weapon). Only one set of pouches was issued, and worn on the left, while a standard three-pocket M1911 cartridge pouch was worn on the right side (the five-round stripper clips could be loaded into the magazine while fitted in the weapon). A small number of early black leather pouches were issued, but most were made of light tan or olive green *Press-Stoff*, or tan or grey canvas with black leather edging and straps. Each pocket was secured by a stud-closed strap and retaining loop. On the back were two belt loops and a belt support strap 'D' ring. (The earlier limited issue Gew.41 (M) and Gew.41 (W) had fixed ten-round magazines filled by 7.92mm loading clips, and individuals armed with them used M1911 cartridge pouches.)

MP43/MP44 magazine pouches

The MP43 machine pistol was introduced in limited numbers in late 1943 to provide an individual automatic weapon with substantially more firepower than existing machine pistols and semi-automatic rifles. Minor modifications were made and full production began in early 1944 of the MP44. It was redesignated the StG44 assault rifle (*Sturmgewehr*) in December 1944 without modification, the new designation being to better differentiate its capabilities from the earlier pistol-calibre machine pistols. The assault rifles were issued principally on the Eastern Front, often with one or two per rifle squad in selected units, especially Panzergrenadiers. There were remote cases of designated assault platoons and companies being predominantly armed with the weapons, but this was seldom. These weapons used a curved 32-round magazine holding the earlier developed 7.92mm short cartridge.

A captured weapons tractor is used to tow a 37mm Pak.35/36 L/45 anti-tank gun of a regimental anti-tank company. The soldiers to its front wear various combinations of field equipment. (Author's collection)

The **assault rifle magazine pouches** (*Sturmgewehr-Magazintaschen*) were similar in design to the second model all-canvas MP40 pouches and worn in the same manner. They consisted of three magazine pockets curved slightly inward, the bases of which were reinforced. Each pocket flap was secured by a stud-closed strap and retaining loop. On the inside edge of the right pouch was a small pocket for the magazine loading device, a small loading clip adapter; the MP43/MP44 used the same five-round loading clip as the Kar.98k. A similar but larger pocket was fitted to the left pouch to accommodate an accessory bag containing small spare parts. (Some late war pouches did not possess these pockets.) The two triple pouch sets were linked together by a thin adjustable web strap intended to be worn around the wearer's back waist; this was often removed. On the back were two angled belt loops and a belt support strap 'D' ring.

Early versions had brown leather pocket flaps, flap securing straps and retaining loops, base reinforcement, accessory pocket flaps, and belt loops. Late war versions usually had these components replaced by canvas and web straps, though the accessory pockets, if present, usually retained the leather flaps. Web flap retaining straps usually had metal tips and inverted 'U' metal retaining brackets. Pouches will be found in olive green, reed green, grey, and light tan, this latter being the most common, and sometimes having a red thread somewhere in the weave.

A fully equipped rifle platoon marches deeper into the USSR past a collection point for captured Soviet machine guns. (Author's collection)

Pistol holsters

A wide variety of **pistol holsters** (*Pistolentaschen*) were issued, often with several versions being found for each model. Captured pistols were also widely used with their accompanying holsters. Pistols were issued, or purchased, accompanied by a holster. Because of the large number of variants holsters will be discussed here only in general terms. The most commonly used pistols were the 9mm Luger P08 and Walther P38, and the 7.65mm Mauser HSc, Walther PP, Walther PPK, and Sauer M38 (H), though many other makes and models were observed. Enlisted men requiring pistols were issued them; these included machine gunners, mortar crewmen, tank and other armoured fighting vehicle crewmen, and others requiring unrestricted movement. Officers were required to purchase their own pistols; those in combat units used the 9mm while many senior officers and those in rear support units and the Replacement Army used 7.65mm models. Overall, the German armed forces used pistols on a wider scale than most other armies.

Holsters were manufactured to accept specified pistol models, whose designations were usually impact or ink stamped inside the flap or back. Most were made of smooth or pebbled black leather, though brown ones will be encountered. Artificial leather and *Press-Stoff* holsters will also be found, as will the odd canvas and leather composite. The typical holster was closed by a large flap to retain and protect the pistol. Most were secured by a strap and stud, either with the strap attached to the holster's body and the stud to the flap or vice versa. Others were secured by a simple stud fitted to the body and a stud hole in the flap, or a strap

and a metal inverted 'U' bracket through which the strap was passed. Most included an integral magazine pocket (most were eight-round) on the side or edge, covered by the pistol's protecting flap. A few versions included a small pocket for a cleaning rod or disassembly/reloading tool, the latter often fitted inside the flap. On the back were one or two belt loops. Very limited use was made of privately purchased separate two-pocket leather magazine pouches for the P08 and P38. Holsters were required to be worn on the left hip with the butt facing forward, though they were sometimes worn on the opposite side.

MG34/MG42 machine gun accessories

The basis for German small unit firepower was the 7.92mm light machine gun (*leichter Machinengewehr*), one of which was issued to each rifle squad in infantry, Panzergrenadier, mountain, and cavalry regiments. These were supplemented by heavy (tripod-mounted) examples of the same machine guns (*schwerer MG*) in the battalion machine gun company. Machine guns were also liberally distributed to reconnaissance, motorcycle rifle, and pioneer units to support direct combat, and to unit headquarters and artillery and support units for self-protection. A number of accessories were issued with the MG34 and MG42:

Each gunner carried an **M1934 replacement parts pouch** (*Ersatzstücketasche 34*) on the right front of his belt; a pistol holster was carried on the left front. The pouch had a rectangular or 'D' ring for the belt support strap on its back. The right support strap was attached to a supplementary loop fitted between the holster's two belt loops or just forward (the buckle end) of the holster. The pouch was a rigid black leather box, usually with reinforcing rivets. To the lid was attached a leather strap that fastened to a stud on the pouch's bottom. On the back were two belt loops and the support strap ring. Sometimes a yellow 'E' was painted on top of the lid (for *Ersatzstücke*— replacement parts). Late war pouches were made of black or light tan *Press-Stoff*. Inside were carried an oil container (with brush inside lid), cleaning brush, small wrench, two bolt assemblies, bolt carrier, firing pin, firing pin lock, and firing pin retainer (the latter items in a small metal spare parts box). An asbestos pad for use when handling hot barrels was usually carried under the securing strap. The MG42 machine gun's spare parts pouch was almost identical to the MG34's, as were the spare parts, tools, and other accessories.

A metal **tool kit case** (*Werkzeugtasche 34*), similar in design to the Kar.98k's M1934 cleaning kit but larger, was also issued. It contained a ruptured cartridge extractor, oil can, plastic sulphur container (mixed with oil as a lubricant), chamber brush, and anti-aircraft ring sight. A similar kit was issued with the MG42.

Several models of **barrel protectors** (*Laufschüter*) were issued to carry spare barrels. These lengthwise-hinged housings were made of steel and fitted with a canvas or web sling (modified leather Kar.98k slings were also used). Machine gunners and assistant gunners carried the allotted spare barrels slung behind the back, two for light machine guns and three for heavy. Heavy MG34 machine gun teams were usually issued the two-barrel carrier. Variants were: *Laufbehälter 34*—two MG34 barrels; *Laufschüter 34*—one MG34 barrel; *Laufschüter 42*—one MG42 barrel; *Laufschüter 43*—one MG34 *or* MG42 barrel.

Other accessories included a metal optical sight carrying case carried by the heavy machine gun team leader by an adjustable web strap; this held the special indirect and direct long-range fire optical sight (with a sight reticle illumination system for night firing). A canvas and webbing **M1934 ammunition carrying bag** (*Munitionstrageerichten 34*) was used to carry a 300-round belt **M1934 and M1941 cartridge containers** (*Patronenkasten 34 und 41*). Two of these were carried together by the aid of a web strap assembly. The steel or aluminium cartridge containers were of several variants with different latches and manufacturing stamping methods. Extra 50-round belt drums (*Gurttrommel 34*) were carried in pairs in a steel basket-type **M1934 belt drum carrier** (*Gurttrommelträger 34*). The above metal items were usually painted olive green, dark yellow, or *Luftwaffe* blue grey. The 75-round saddle drum magazine (*Patronentrommel 34*), requiring the fitting of a modified feed-cover, was no longer used after 1940 due to feed problems.

Grenade accessories

The standard rifle grenade launcher was a 3cm cup-type discharge launcher (*Gewehrgranate Schiessbacher*) designed for the Kar.98k carbine and similar weapons. Issued on the basis of one per squad in combat units, it and its accessories were carried in a **rifle grenade pouch** (*Gewehrgranatetasche*). This was a deep tapered pouch made of black leather, olive green or reed green canvas, or black *Press-Stoff* (late war). The flap was secured by a stud and strap held down by a retaining loop. On both sides were a 'D' ring strap to attach the adjustable carrying strap; on the back was a single wide-angled belt loop. Late war pouches had the carrying strap permanently fastened. Inside were carried the cup-type launcher, launcher sight, disassembly tool, and cup cleaning tool. It was slung over the right shoulder with the pouch at the left hip; if attached to the belt it would be on the left hip angled with the top forward. Though little used, a second type of grenade launcher was also carried in this pouch. The rifle grenade launcher for armour combat (*Gewehrgranate zur Panzerbekämpfung 40*) was a spigot-type discharge launcher intended only to launch a large anti-tank grenade. With it was issued a folding auxiliary direct fire sight and no special tools.

Rifle grenades were carried in one of two types of double canvas carriers; both consisted of two flat bags with a flap secured by a strap and buckle. The two bags of the earlier **carrying**

A rifle squad prepare to attack during Operation Blau, USSR, July 1942. The man closest to the camera has an M1934 machine gun single barrel protector slung across his back. (US Army)

pouches for rifle grenades (*Tragetaschen für Gewehrgranaten*) were connected by two adjustable web straps attached to the edges and worn around the wearer's back; a long adjustable strap, attached to the tops, went round the neck. The flap securing straps were leather. The later **pair of carrying bags for rifle grenades** (*Paar Tragbeutel für Gewehrgranaten*) was designed to be hand-carried only. Of similar design, it lacked the back and shoulder straps, the two bags being held together by a single thin canvas hand-carrying strap. Its flap securing straps were made of webbing. Both types are generally found in field grey, reed green, and brown shades. Inside were carried the many varied types of 3cm rifle grenades and their launching cartridges. They were also used to carry stick hand grenades.

Stick hand grenades (*Stielhandgranaten*) were carried on the person in all manner of locations: in the boot tops, belt, tunic front, strapped to entrenching tool carriers, in other containers, etc. The simple **carrying pouches for hand grenades** (*Tragetaschen für Handgranaten*) were used to a limited extent. Similar to the carrying pouches for rifle grenades, these consisted of two green, tan, or brown coarse-weave cloth bags fitted with two canvas straps, one worn round the neck and the other behind the small of the back. Four or five stick grenades were carried in each of the drawstring-closed bags. Similar carriers locally fabricated from sandbags were also used. A pull-over hand grenade vest saw extremely limited issue; made of field grey fabric, it was fitted with five deep strap-secured vertical grenade pockets on both the front and back.

Light mortar accessories

The 5cm light mortar M1936 (*leichter Granatwerfer 36 — lGrW36*) was originally issued on the basis of one per mortar section in infantry rifle platoons, as well as to reconnaissance and motorcycle rifle units. This heavy and complex little weapon was withdrawn from service in 1942, principally due to its limited down-range effect, weight, and deployment difficulties.

The key accessory of interest for this weapon is the **M1939 carrying harness** (*Traggestell 39*); three of these were issued to the mortar crew to carry the barrel, base plate, and ten-round ammunition cases. It consisted of a black tubular steel triangular-shaped pack frame with a unique folding support shelf and fitted with web shoulder, securing, and waist straps. Its shoulder straps were attached to the wearer's belt. The canvas bag for the combat pack (*Beutel zum Gefechtsgepäck*) — described under 'Basic Equipment' with the combat pack — was issued with the frame. Small numbers of these were issued to infantry units in lieu of the web combat pack ('A' frame) in 1939. These were modified by the removal of the integral shoulder straps and fitting of hooked 'D' rings to permit the frame to be attached to the belt support straps.

Flare pistol accessories

There were two versions of the standard Army model flare pistol (*Leuchtpistole-Heeres Modell* — also known as a *Signalpistole*): the short- (*mit kurzem Lauf*) and long-barrel (*mit langem Lauf*). The short-barrel version of this 2.7cm flare pistol had been in use since 1928 while the long-barrel was adopted in 1935. Several other flare pistols were in limited use, such as the M1942 (*Leuchtpistole 42 — LeuP42*), along with captured and World War I models. The battle pistol (*Kampfpistole*) and assault pistol (*Sturmpistole*) were modifications of the *Leuchtpistole mit kurzem Lauf* that fired casualty-producing rounds. A rifled barrel-liner insert was provided which, when removed, would permit the firing of pyrotechnic rounds.

Both versions were provided a black leather **signal pistol holster** (*Signalpistolentasche*) not unlike those used for standard pistols. This was closed by a flap secured by a strap and inverted 'U' ring. A belt loop was fitted on the back, and a thin detachable leather shoulder carrying strap was also provided. A cleaning rod was attached to the holster by a carbine hook.

An extremely wide variety of 2.7cm pyrotechnic rounds were available. These were carried in two types of **signal cartridge pouches** (*Signalpatronentasche*). The large (*grosse*) version was a rectangular box holding 18 rounds in three rows of loops, closed by a lid secured by two straps and studs; a narrow detachable leather carrying strap was attached to the ends. These were made of black leather, *Press-Stoff*, and olive green canvas. The small (*kleine*) black leather version held 12 rounds in two rows of loops; it too was closed by two straps and studs and had a detachable carrying strap, and was additionally fitted with two belt loops.

The first Russian winter. An MG34 heavy machine gun crew searches their sector of fire. The gunner's pistol holster is clearly visible as is the squad leader's MP40 machine pistol and universal binocular container. (Author's collection)

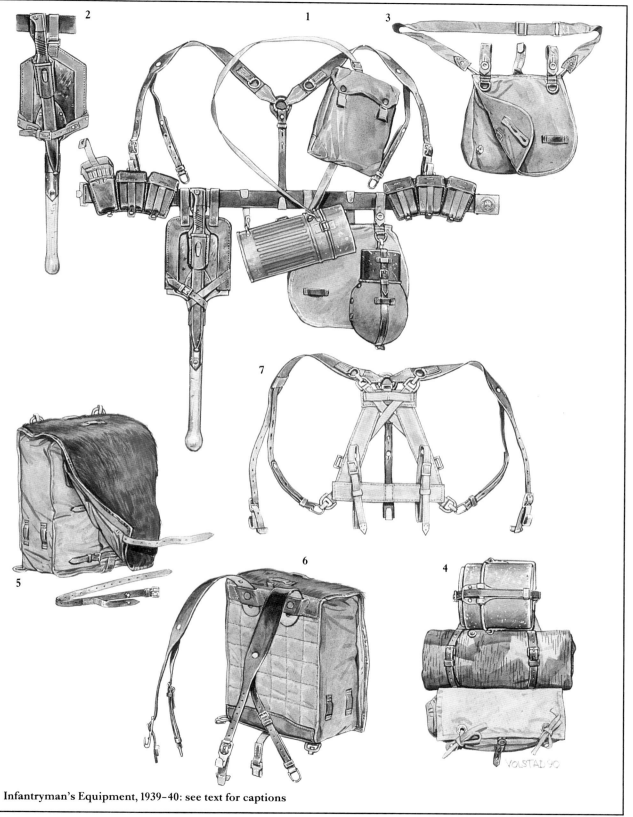

Infantryman's Equipment, 1939–40: see text for captions

A

Infantryman's and Troop Leader's Equipment, 1939–41: see text for captions

B

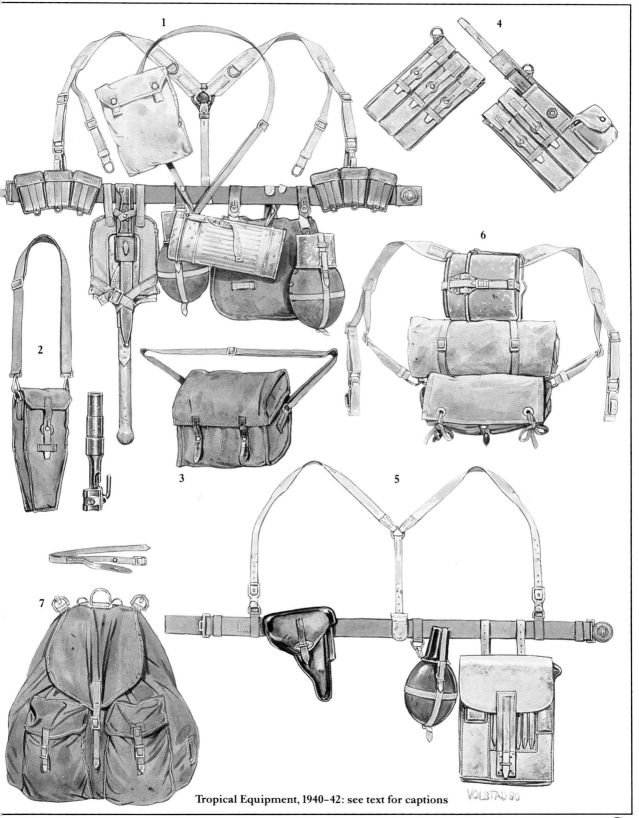

Tropical Equipment, 1940–42: see text for captions

VOLSTAD 90

C

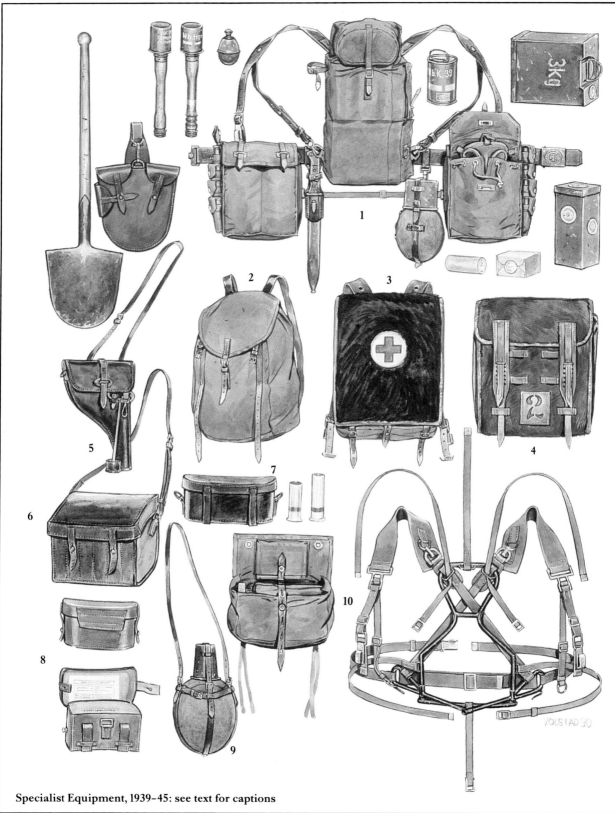

Specialist Equipment, 1939–45: see text for captions

D

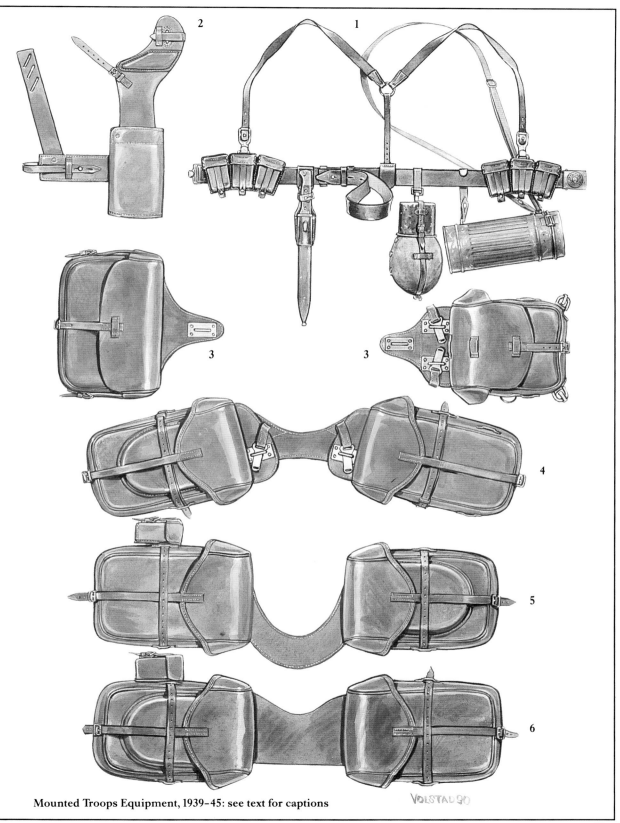

Mounted Troops Equipment, 1939–45: see text for captions

VOLSTAD 90

E

Mountain Troops Equipment, 1939–45: see text for captions

F

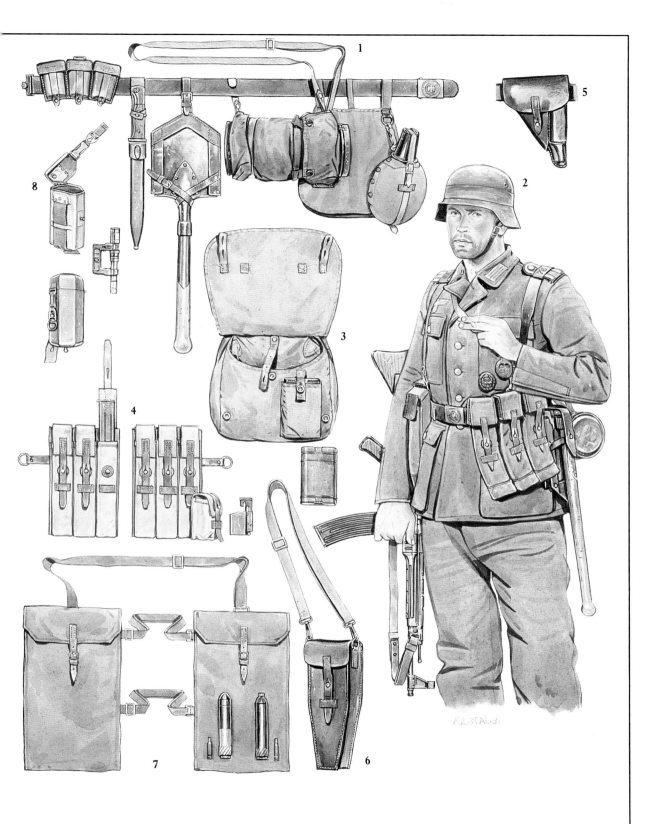

Infantry Equipment, 1942–44: see text for captions

Infantry Equipment, 1943–45: see text for captions

H

Weapon slings

Most weapon **carrying slings** (*Trageriemen*) were made of brown or black leather, though use was made of olive green and tan webbing. Leather slings were predominantly used with rifles and machine guns while webbing ones were generally fitted to machine pistols and assault rifles. All were generally constructed as a one-piece adjustable type with a single metal slide buckle, though some used a locking-type buckle. Black or brown leather slings for the MG34/MG42 tripod had a triangular ring and carbine hook fitted on both ends. Two straps were required to carry the tripod (*Lafette 34 oder 42*). The load-bearing portions of these slings were wider than normal, and tapered to normal width at the ends. Modified machine gun and rifle slings were often used in lieu of these.

A large heavy-duty **hauling sling** (*Schleppriemen*) was issued to anti-tank and infantry gun crews to aid in the manhandling of these weapons. They were made of black leather or heavy tan canvas and fitted with an adjustment buckle and large carbine hook to fasten to the weapon. They were worn over whichever shoulder was appropriate.

SPECIALIST EQUIPMENT

A wide range of specialised equipment was issued to selected individuals due to their duty requirements, the environment they operated in, or their transportation. A fine and sometimes blurred line exists between what can be considered individual equipment and unit equipment. This latter was usually issued by the unit, or purchased by officers in some cases, and its allocation was strictly controlled by authorisation tables.

Troop leaders' equipment

Troop leaders' equipment (*Ausrüstung des Truppenführer*—both officers and NCOs in leadership positions) included several items designed to accommodate their duties. Officers were required to purchase many of these items. Officers and others of equivalent rank (Defence Forces officials; special leaders; postal, medical and veterinary officers; music masters and inspectors; senior ensigns—officer candidates; and clergy) were required to wear an **M1934 belt with shoulder strap** (*Leibriemen mit Schulterriemen 34*) with all classes of uniform[1]. It was a light reddish brown, the same as officers' horse tack. A thin line or groove was pressed around the edges of the belt and shoulder strap on most versions. Armour officers were ordered to wear a black version with the black *Panzer* uniform, but most retained the brown. Adopted in May 1934 to replace the similar *Reichswehr* model used since 1930, it was composed of a 5cm wide waist belt (5.5cm wide belts were also authorised) and a 'Sam Browne'-type shoulder strap. In May 1943 the width was reduced to 4.5cm, though wider belts could be used until worn out. The buckle was an open-faced frame and prong style made of matt aluminium; matt gold coloured for generals and equivalents. The two-piece adjustable shoulder strap was 2.5cm wide and fitted with a carbine hook on both ends; these attached to two stud-secured leather belt loops with 'D' rings positioned on the belt at the left front, with the strap running over the right shoulder, and the right rear. Though principally ornamental, the strap did serve to support any attached equipment, usually a sidearm (pistol, sabre, dagger). The shoulder strap's buckles and carbine hooks and the belt buckle were finely pebble-finished. In November 1939 it was directed that regimental commanders and below in combat units of the Field Army would wear the enlisted man's black belt and buckle; this order was seldom obeyed due to the status German officers placed on the traditional brown belt as a sign of authority. In July 1943 it was ordered that the brown officers' belts be dyed black and all new ones manufactured in black.

An officers' **tropical belt** (*tropisch Leibriemen*) saw very

[1] Except with the parade uniform, for which a special brocade dress belt (*Feldbinde*) with a circular buckle was required.

This machine gunner's equipment is composed of the support straps for infantry, belt, late model P38 pistol holster, small entrenching tool and carrier, M1931 bread bag, M1931 field flask, and M1934 machine gun repair parts pouch. (Troy Haley Collection)

limited use in North Africa. It consisted of a reed green or tan web waist belt fitted with an olive green-painted circular officers' parade belt buckle. Most officers preferred to wear their standard brown leather belt in North Africa, however.

In late September 1939 the shoulder strap was forbidden for wear by regimental commanders and below within the Field Army, in an effort to prevent them from being identified at a distance; in late November its wear by any officer was prohibited. In its place infantry lieutenants were authorised to wear the standard belt support straps with auxiliary straps, like their troops. Captains and higher of Field Army infantry regiments were authorised either the **support straps for cartridge pouches** (*Trageriemen für Partonentaschen*) or **cavalry supports** (*Kavallerie-Tragegurt*) to support their field equipment. These were seldom worn, though, as it was considered a lowering of officers' status. These support strap assemblies were almost identical. They were composed of two narrow adjustable front straps fixed to an 'O' ring, sometimes padded; to this was fixed a short back strap. This was attached to the back centre of the waist belt by a hook, while the front straps were hooked directly to the belt or supplementary loops. There were no auxiliary straps. The 'cavalry supports' front straps were straight, while the 'support straps for cartridge pouches' were wider at the shoulders and tapered to the same width as the cavalry straps; they also had a protective leather tab fixed to the rear belt hook. These supports were also issued to non-infantry and cavalry units respectively in lieu of the belt supports with auxiliary straps issued to the infantry and some other combat units. In April 1940 the support straps for cartridge pouches were redesignated **belt supports for officers** (*Koppeltraggestell für Offiziere*) and the cavalry supports became **belt supports for cavalry** (*Koppeltraggestell*

für Kavallerie) in order to better describe their current function.

Sidearms (*Seitengewehr*) included pistols, bayonets, sabres and daggers. The Army dagger was adopted in 1935 for wear by officers and designated special rank categories. Its authorisation for wear was rescinded in 1944, along with the wearing of sabres. Daggers and sabres were attached to the belt by various hangers and frogs. They are not discussed here as they were not field equipment.

The **M1935 report/map case** (*Meldekartentasche 35*), usually called a map or dispatch case by collectors, was widely issued to officers and senior NCOs in unit leadership positions, artillery observers, selected signalmen, military policemen, messengers and others. It replaced a similar model used by the *Reichswehr* from the 1920s. Made of smooth or pebbled black or brown leather, there were many variants. Some were made in the officer's reddish brown colour. They were occasionally painted field grey or green during the war. Late war versions were made of artificial leather or *Press-Stoff*. They were commonly constructed of a flat case closed by a flap; under the flap were seven pencil pockets alongside one or two ruler pockets. The case was divided inside into two compartments by a leather divider. Most had a flap covering the upper third to half of the case's depth, though there were also full-flap variants. The flap was secured either by strap and buckle, or a strap and inverted 'U' and slotted metal plate fastener. On the upper back were two leather belt loops, and most had a detachable or fixed adjustable shoulder strap; they could be attached directly to the belt or slung over the right shoulder, in both cases being worn on the left side or front. A map protection cover (*Kartenschultzhülle*), composed of two panels of clear celluloid joined by a leather frame, was included, in which place a folded map. A wide variety of items might be carried in the despatch/map case: report forms, maps, notebook, message pad, lead and grease pencils, ink pens, eraser, rulers, scales, protractor, grid co-ordinate scale, map distance measuring device, small drafting triangle, march compass, etc. Besides issue cases, similar commercially made models were also privately purchased by officers; and use was made of captured map cases—something of a status symbol.

Service binoculars (*Doppelfernrohr* also *Dienstglas, Doppelglas*) were issued to officers, some NCOs, artillery observers, aircraft spotters, etc. The standard issue **universal binoculars** (*Einheits-Doppelfernrohr*) were 6 × 30 (6 power, 30 degree field of vision) and adopted in the mid-1930s. They replaced a number of earlier models, which generally remained in use, alongside privately purchased makes. The universal model was made by different well-known optics manfacturers and many variants existed. Earlier versions had the metal parts black lacquered, the optical bodies being covered with thin artificial leather or synthetic rubber, both black with a pebbled finish. From 1943 they were also painted dark yellow without any form of body covering. A thin black real or artificial leather carrying strap was attached. To protect the eyepieces, an oval protector (*Regenschutzdeckel*) made of black leather, synthetic rubber, or Bakelite was provided; this was attached to the carrying strap by small loops. A black leather button hanger (*Behälter*) was provided; this fastened around the rear binocular body connecting arm and was buttoned to an upper tunic button. The eyepiece protector and button flap were used when the binoculars were carried around the neck.

The **binocular container** (*Doppelfernrohr Behälter*) was of the usual kidney-shaped cross-section and made of real or artificial black leather, black or light tan *Press-Stoff* or black Bakelite. The lid was secured by an elastic or spring-loaded fastener similar to that of the gas mask case. An adjustable, detachable black leather carrying strap was attached to 'D' rings on the container's sides; two narrow or one wide belt loops were

fixed on the back surface.

Officers, NCOs, and many enlisted men were provided or purchased a small flashlight or torch; prior to the war all personnel were issued one. Many different commercial models, most similar to the standard issue, were used alongside captured ones. The issue **field pocket lamp** (*Feldtaschen Lampe*) was a small field grey or grey painted metal rectangular flat box with a round clear lens in the upper front. There were three slots near the bottom front, each with a small colour-coded slide knob; these permitted a blue, red, or green plastic filter to be slid over the bulb. The on/off knob was on the bottom. At the top and bottom of the back were small leather tabs with a buttonhole for attaching the lamp to the tunic.

Mounted troops' equipment

Mounted troops included cavalry, mounted rifles, mounted artillery, and cavalry reconnaissance units, as well as designated mounted officers and other individuals in infantry units (this practice was eliminated early in the war). German horse tack, **equipment for troop service horses** (*Ausrüstung des Truppendienstpferdes*) or simply 'horse equipment' (*Pferdeausrüstung*), included the lightweight **M1925 Army saddle** (*Armeesattel 25*) with open steel stirrups, double reins (*Kandarenzügel*), and bit and single-snaffle bridle (*Zäumung auf Kandare*). This tack was dark brown for enlisted men and light reddish brown for officers. The **saddle blanket** (*Satteldecke*) was of dark grey wool and was additionally used to cover the horse in inclement weather; it measured about 225 × 195cm (7 ft. 7 in. × 6 ft. 4 in.) and folded in quarters when placed under the saddle. Belt support straps for cavalry are described above under 'Troop Leaders' Equipment'. A complete set of horse equipment, tack and baggage weighed in excess of 45kg, over 100 pounds.

The **M1934 saddle bags**, or pack cases (*Packtaschen 34*), were issued to mounted enlisted men in lieu of packs. (Some use was made of saddle bags by crews of motorcycles, which were also

Assault troops attack a Stalingrad tractor factory, 1942. All are carrying combat packs. The man closest to the camera has two M1939 stick hand grenades secured to his folding entrenching tool carrier. (US Army)

equipped with specially designed side bags.) These were composed of two differently designed brown leather bags, the right or rider's baggage (*Reitergepäck*) and the left or horse's baggage (*Pferdegepäck*), connected by a leather saddle connector (*Sattelüberwurf*). The pack lids were closed by a buckled strap. On the front of the horse pack was a semicircular pocket closed by the pack lid. An extension of the pack backing protruded above the lids, on which were a slotted metal plate and metal tipped leather strap to secure the packs to the connector. The connector was fitted with two metal plates riveted to both ends; one had a metal inverted 'U' bracket that fitted through the slotted plate on the packs to be secured by the packs' metal tipped strap; the other plates each had three slots—one was selected to permit the rider sufficient knee clearance, and was fitted to an inverted 'U' bracket on the saddle. Straps on the connector, fitted with carbine hooks, were passed through the brackets to secure the entire assemblage to the saddle.

The rider's pack could be worn as a backpack when operating dismounted. It was fitted with two leather shoulder straps that attached to 'D' rings on the pack's bottom; when attached to the saddle these straps were tightened to be kept out of the way. This pack was also fitted with three leather loops, one on each side and one on the top, through which **greatcoat straps for mounted troops** (*Mantelriemen für Berittenen Truppen*) were secured. These brown leather straps were similar to the greatcoat straps for foot troops (described under 'Basic Equipment' with the greatcoat roll), but lacked the buttoning strap. The cook pot was removed from the horse's bag and attached to the outside of the rider's bag when carried as a backpack; this applied to all models of dismountable saddle bags. It was very common for cook pots to

A late war rucksack for artillery, olive green with black leather fittings. Its right shoulder strap is fitted with a hook used as a quick-release. (Troy Haley collection)

be attached outside a saddle bag and the extra bag space used for other items. Field flasks and other equipment items were also often attached to the saddle or saddle bags rather than carried on the rider.

In the rider's pack (right) were carried: laced top shoes, undershirt, socks, swimming shorts (used when bathing the horse), shaving kit, washing kit, sewing kit, cleaning brush, tent line, and a half iron ration. Inside the horse pack (left) were: cook pot, grooming brush, curry comb, and blanket strap (used to secure the saddle blanket as a horse cover). In the outside pocket were two horseshoes, nails, studs, stud calk (a spanner-like tool), and tethering ring.

On the back of the saddle was strapped the **rear baggage** (*Hintergepäck*): a greatcoat and/or blanket and tent quarter, plus canvas corn bag and a collapsible canvas water bucket packed in tubular grey canvas case. It was secured to the saddle by two side and one middle pack straps (*Seiten- und Mittelpackriemen*), brown leather with two buckles, attached to three rings on the saddle's cantle (hind-bow).

In February 1940 **new type saddle bags** (*Packtaschen neuer art—n/A*) were introduced, though the M1934 remained in wide use. Its purpose was to permit additional items to be carried both mounted and dismounted. Unlike all previous saddle bags, this model was carried behind the saddle and the bags were of different sizes.

The small (*kleine Packtasche*) was attached on the right side and contained the rider's baggage. It comprised a rectangular brown leather box closed by a strap and buckle-secured flap that covered the upper half of the front. Leather loops were sewn to the sides to attach the greatcoat roll, and two loops on the flap's front allowed attachment of the cook pot when the bag was worn as a dismounted backpack. To permit this, two adjustable leather shoulder straps were fitted to the pack's back and attached to hooked 'D' rings on its bottom. Other 'D' rings were fitted to attach the auxiliary straps. A leather extension of the pack's back

(folded down when worn as a backpack) protruded above, and was fitted with three slotted metal plates and short straps, which served to fasten it to the saddle. An exterior pocket was fitted to the lower half of the pack's front and was just covered by the pack flap. Inside were carried a half iron ration, 15 rounds reserve ammunition, carbine cleaning kit, undershirt, gloves, washing kit, shaving kit, cleaning utensils, and tent line.

The large pack (*grosse Packtasche*), carried on the left side, contained the horse baggage. It was the same depth as the small pack, but wider, and the interior was divided into three compartments; there was no pocket on the front. The lid was secured by three buckled straps, one on the front and one each side. The back extension had only one slotted metal saddle attachment plate. The cook pot was carried in the large compartment with the horseshoes and accessories, horse brush, curry comb, and blanket strap in the two smaller ones.

Two earlier models of saddle bags were used to a limited extent by cavalry training units early in the war, but were eventually replaced by the M1934 bags. The **M1926 saddle bags** (*Packtaschen 26*) were an interim model possessing the characteristics of the M1934 and the old type saddle bags (see below). A narrow arch-shaped leather connector held the two bags together. The left (rider's) bag could be detached and worn as a backpack. A horseshoe pocket was sewn to the outside of the right (horse's) bag, and a pouch, closed by a strap and buckle-secured lid, was attached to the forward, or left, side of the rider's bag. In this was placed the odd combination of a shaving kit and reserve ammunition. Other contents were similar to the M1934.

The earlier **old type saddle bags** (*Packtaschen alter Art — a/A*) had been used since World War I; though similar to the M1926 bags, there were some distinct differences. Firstly the right bag, rather than the left, contained the rider's baggage while the left contained the horse's, the reverse practice of all subsequent models. The leather connector was much wider, the horseshoe pocket was on the left (horse's) bag, and the right (rider's) bag was not detachable as a backpack. The side pouch (for shaving kit and reserve ammunition) was in the same position as on the M1926, but this placed it on the horse's bag. In March 1932 it was directed that the right (rider's) bag be modified to permit its use as a backpack; this was not always accomplished, however. The bag's contents were similar to the M1926's.

A **carbine carrying device** (*Karabinertragevorrichtung*) was used by the cavalry and other mounted units, but after the outbreak of war it was far more common, and practical, for the carbine to be slung diagonally across the rider's back. The carbine shoe (*Karabinerschuh*) was composed of a butt pocket with two extensions to which securing straps were fixed, all of brown leather to match the saddle. This device was attached to the lower left rear side of the saddle. The rider attached a black leather (to match the belt) carbine holder sling (*Karabiner-halteriemen*) to his waist belt by the means of two belt loops. The sling was then formed into a loop by securing it to a stud fitted on one end, and attached to the carbine's sling. The carbine's butt was then placed in the carbine shoe attached to the saddle and the forearm placed through the looped sling. In order to use the carbine, the rider could either unfasten the looped sling and bring the weapon to his shoulder, or he would have to withdraw the carbine from the shoe by raising it vertically, lower it toward the ground to clear the looped sling, and then bring it to his shoulder.

Prior to the war enlisted cavalrymen were issued a **carrying strap for enlisted man's sabre** (*Trageriemen zum Mann-schaftssäbel*). This was an adjustable black or brown leather strap

A colonel general and Panzer lieutenant colonel confer over a map. Both have binoculars slung around their necks. The staff officer has the 6 × 30 universal binoculars with the eyepiece protector attached to the carrying strap. His belt shoulder strap is plainly visible. The general has an older model of binoculars. (Author's collection)

with a double rectangular ring on the upper end and a carbine hook on the lower. Fixed to the rectangular ring was a short nickel chain also fitted with a carbine hook. The sabre was attached to the strap and chain carbine hooks and the entire assembly fastened to an inverted supplementary loop on the waist belt's left hip. This device was used only when dismounted. When mounted, enlisted men attached the sabre to the saddle's right rear when carrying a carbine and to the left rear when not, as did officers at all times. Sabres were not authorised in the field after December 1940, but were again permitted in 1943 for cavalry, though seldom carried.

Artillery troops' equipment

The artillery troops employed all sorts of cases and pouches to carry sights, aiming circles, quadrants, range finders, etc.; these are beyond the scope of this book, as they were weapon systems equipment.

The **rucksack for artillery** (*Rucksack für Artillerie*) was introduced in February 1940 for dismounted artillery personnel, replacing the M1934 pack; mounted personnel used saddle bags. These also saw limited issue to infantry and other units from 1941, especially on the Eastern Front and in North Africa, the latter issued in reed green or tan. In January 1943 they were

This rifle platoon leader's equipment consists of: enlisted man's belt (officers in combat units were authorised to wear it, but more often retained the brown officer's belt), M1935 report/map case, M1931 field flask attached to an inverted

supplementary loop, and universal binocular container. Above are a march compass, field pocket lamp (one of many military-style private purchase models) and 6 × 30 universal binoculars. (Troy Haley collection)

authorised for cyclist units. This simple one-compartment rectangular canvas bag was usually in olive green, but later ones were also made in grey, brown, and tan shades. The top opening was secured by a drawstring; a canvas flap, fastened by a leather strap and buckle, further closed the rucksack. Web shoulder straps were fixed to the upper back centre. The left strap attached to a buckle fitted on the lower left corner while the right had a carbine snap that fastened to a 'D' ring on the lower right corner, to provide for quick release. Most were fitted with two buckled leather straps on the front just below the mouth to attach a rolled tent quarter.

In about 1943 (perhaps earlier) a version was issued without the integral shoulder straps, designed to be attached to the belt support straps for infantry like the M1939 and combat pack. Two hooked 'D' rings were fixed at the upper corners for attachment to the support straps' shoulder-mounted 'D' rings; two more were placed at the lower corners for the auxiliary straps. Items carried in the rucksack were similar to the contents of the standard infantryman's packs.

Pioneer troops' equipment

In March 1941 a special **pioneer assault pack** (*Pioniersturmgepäck*) was introduced. This ensemble was composed of an assault pouch (*Sturmtasche*), two different side pouches (*Seitettaschen*), and the belt supports for infantry (*Koppeltraggestell für*

Infanterie—described in 'Basic Equipment' under the belt supports), all coupled together by the standard waist belt. It was authorised on the basis of one per five pioneers in divisional pioneer battalions. It was analogous to the infantry's combat pack and those issued it were permitted to retain their M1939 pack, though the latter could not be worn with this ensemble and was carried in unit transport. Between the assault pouch and side pouches there was little space left on the waist belt to attach other equipment, such as the bread bag and entrenching tool, though the field flask and bayonet could be accommodated. The pouches were made of olive green or light brown canvas and all straps were web. Production of the pioneer assault pack ceased in 1944.

The assault pouch was composed of three compartments. The upper one was for the cook pot, which was placed in the upside-down compartment, folded over with the cook pot on its side, and secured by a strap to a buckle fitted on the centre compartment; a tie string additionally secured the cook pot in the compartment. The two lower compartments had side-opening flaps on the right side, secured by straps passed through inverted 'U' shaped brackets and rectangular metal eyelets. The centre compartment was designed to hold two NbK39 smoke pots and the lower one a 3kg demolition charge. On the pouch's corners were fixed hooked 'D' rings to attach it to the belt support straps.

The side pouches were of different designs, but both possessed a top opening flap secured by two web straps fastened by inverted 'U' shaped brackets and rectangular metal eyelets. The two pouches were connected by an adjustable web strap worn behind the small of the back. Both also had four snap-fastened cartridge pockets on the front edges (the edges facing toward the wearer's mid-section), each holding a single five-round carbine loading clip. The left pouch was divided into two compartments for stick and 'egg' hand grenades and other items as required. The right pouch had a single rubber-lined compartment for small demolition charges (M1928 100g boring cartridges, M1928 200g and M1924 1kg demolition charges). On its front was a pocket closed by a flap and one strap for the standard gas mask, also secured by a drawstring. On the pouches' backs were web belt loops and support strap attachment rings.

Several carriers were designed to accommodate pioneer tools, made of real or artificial leather or canvas. Most of these tools had detachable handles for ease of carrying. Long-handle pioneer spades and pickaxes were provided with a carrying case for their blades/heads which incorporated attachment straps for their handles. The short wire cutters and hatchet were both provided with leather belt pouches. The long wire cutters had a leather-reinforced canvas belt pouch. The pioneer hand saw used a leather belt scabbard fitted with a bayonet scabbard retaining loop, the bayonet frog being attached to the belt beside the saw scabbard; it was worn in place of the entrenching tool. Several types of leather or canvas cases were provided to carry demolition accessories and charges.

Mountain troops' equipment

Mountain troops were issued a variety of specialised items, including climbing pitons, carabiners, hard-lay rope, and ava-lanche marker cords and flags. High mountain troops were issued ice axes, and ten-point crampons for attachment to boots when ice-climbing. Mountain troops, designated ski units, and speci-ally trained infantry units were outfitted with snow skis, ski poles, and various types of snow-shoes.

While a number of rucksacks were used in the course of the war, the standard model was the **M1931 rucksack for high mountain troops** (*Rucksack 31 für Hochgebirgstruppen*). This was a ruggedly constructed bergen-type rucksack made of olive green canvas with black or brown leather straps, fittings, and edge bindings. It had a single large compartment closed by a drawstring and a flap secured by three straps and buckles. Inside, on the back, was a large pocket closed by a flap with three buttoned straps; this was for small personal items such as the washing, shaving, and sewing kits. On the underside of the main compartment flap was a small accessory pocket secured by three small buckled straps. On the outside of the flap were four small leather equipment attachment loops. Three greatcoat roll retain-ing loops were fitted to the flap at top centre and both sides near the bottom. An external pocket was sewn to both sides and closed

by a buckled strap and flap. On the front centre was a larger pocket secured by two buckled straps and a flap. All of the flaps were edged with leather binding. Two large 'D' rings were fastened to a leather patch at the rucksack's upper centre back, to which were attached leather shoulder straps fitted with belt hooks for attachment to the cartridge pouches or supplementary loops. Auxiliary straps were fastened by carbine hooks to 'D' rings fixed on the shoulder strap; they were fastened in turn to buckles on the rucksack's lower corners. Four accessory and two shoe bags, all of linen and closed by drawstrings, were issued with the rucksack; these sometimes bore coloured (light green, light blue, gold-yellow, red) cloth triangles as a coding system to identify contents. Wartime M1931 rucksacks were simplified, with only two flap straps, differently arranged interior pockets, canvas shoulder straps, no side pockets, or only two pockets on the front. Besides contents similar to the standard packs, mountain troops carried the necessary cold weather clothing and additional rations, since they often could not be resupplied daily by unit field kitchens.

From late 1941 it was directed that **battle rucksacks** (*Kampf Rucksacken*) be issued to infantry units on the Eastern Front in lieu of the M1934/M1939 packs; like mountain troops, infantry units in the East needed to carry additional clothing and rations. They also saw use in North Africa. No single standard design was developed, but rather a number of different Bergen-type ruck-sacks were fielded to meet the sudden need. They were made by companies which had manufactured commercial rucksacks prior to the war and adapted their existing designs.

Outwardly these rucksacks were similar to the M1931, but usually less robust in construction and lacking some of the amenities, with those of late war production being rather crude. They were usually made of olive green, reed green, grey, brown, or tan canvas. Flap securing straps were usually of black or brown leather as were other fittings. Most had two pockets with flaps

One of many variants of a late war battle rucksack, olive green with black leather fittings. This *model was designed to be attached to support straps for infantry. (Troy Haley collection)*

secured by buckled straps on the front. The main compartment flap was secured by one or two buckled straps, the opening being further closed by a drawstring. Most had flaps with canvas edge binding, but leather binding was also used. Many had equipment and greatcoat roll attaching loops on the sides and main compartment flap. Some were fitted with leather or canvas shoulder straps attached by various arrangements of hooked 'D' rings, carbine hooks, and buckles, some with quick-release

Another late war variant battle rucksack, dark grey with black leather fittings. This one is slightly more sophisticated than the previous model and has integral shoulder straps, the left one of which is fitted with a carbine hook for quick-release. (Troy Haley collection)

buckles. Others were issued without shoulder straps and were fitted with hooked 'D' rings at the upper back centre and lower corners for attachment to the support straps for infantry, in the same manner as the M1939 pack. In late 1942 a white snow camouflage rucksack cover was issued in conjunction with the new winter suit.

Some mountain units were issued a special **flask for mountain troops** (*Flasche für Gebirgstruppen*), though many used the standard M1931 field flask; in about 1943 production of this large flask was halted and M1931 flasks were issued in their place. It held 1 litre (about 34 ounces) and was of a similar design to the M1931. A carbine hook was fastened to a buckled vertical strap which was fastened around the bottom, running up the front and back to secure the cup in place. The screw cap was secured to this by an extension of the vertical securing strap. The round cup, with two small securing strap brackets, and strap buckles were painted black.

Signal troops' equipment

Signal units were issued a specially designed series of **radio packs** (*Fernsprechtornister*) as unit equipment to carry signals equipment and tools and not issued to individuals to carry personal items. They were available in three models, which appeared the same externally except for a brown leather square sewn near the bottom of the unshaven calfskin-covered lower flap section. Cut out of this in a stencil-like pattern was '1', '2', or '3' to indicate the specific model. The interiors had different arrangements of compartments and securing loops to accommodate their specific contents. The bodies were made of brown canvas. The flap was a two-part design with the upper and lower sections opening outward to allow unrestricted access to the contents. The flaps were secured by two adjustable leather straps fastened by smaller straps passed through inverted metal 'U' shaped brackets that fitted through slots cut in the large straps.

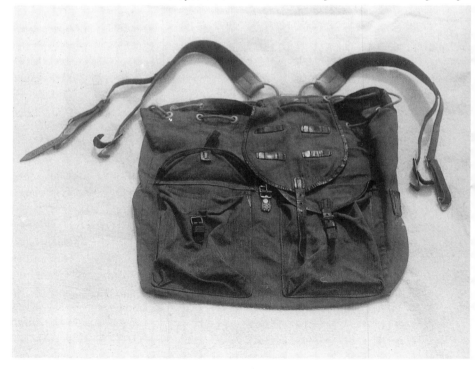

Leather shoulder straps were fixed to the pack's back. Several leather equipment retaining loops were fixed to the lower flap section and pack sides.

Medical troops' equipment

Medical troops were issued a wide range of pouches and cases in which to carry medical supplies and materials. Medical orderlies (*Sanitäter*) at company level were infantrymen with additional basic medical training. Fully trained medical personnel were found only at regimental level and in dedicated medical units at division and higher levels.

Unit medical orderlies were issued two identical **dismounted medical pouches** (*Sanitätstaschen für Unberittene*). These were composed of a rigid brown or black leather rectangular box closed by a lid secured by a tab on both ends that fastened to a stud. The lid was fastened to the front by a sewn leather hinge permitting it to be opened away from the wearer's body. On the back were two leather belt loops and a rectangular ring for fastening belt support straps. Inside were carried field dressings, gauze pads and rolls, tape, tourniquets, antiseptics, and other simple medical supplies. A packing diagram and contents list was pasted to the inside of the lid. There was also a little used **large medical pouch** (*Sanitäts-Grossetaschen*) of almost identical design to the above, but about a quarter larger and lacking the belt supports attachment ring.

The saddle bag-type and more elaborate **mounted medical pack cases** (*Sanitäts Packtaschen für Berittene*) were issued to cavalry and other mounted units' medical orderlies. They were also taught basic first aid for treating wounded/injured horses. These pouches were attached to the rear sides of the saddle in the same manner as the new type saddle bags. Both were made of brown leather and closed by lids that opened away from the saddle and fastened on the sides by tabs and studs. The left case had integral leather shoulder straps, allowing it to be carried dismounted as a backpack; it held medical supplies similar to the dismounted medical pouches'. The right case was larger and held medical supplies for horses, principally in the form of large gauze pads and rolls with cloth bandages. Mounted medical orderlies were also generally issued dismounted medical pouches.

The **M1934 medical pack** (*Sanitätstornister 34*) was issued on the basis of one per company-sized unit to carry additional and reserve medical supplies. Externally it was the same as the standard M1934 pack with the addition of a white leather disc, embroidered with a red cross, sewn to the centre of the ponyhide flap. It had fixed shoulder straps for attachment to the belt. The interior was divided into compartments to hold medical supplies and basic instruments. A rucksack version, the *Sanitätsrucksack*, was issued in about 1942 (perhaps earlier). It was similar to the M1931 rucksack, but with the leather red cross on a white disc sewn to the flap and several compartments and pockets provided inside.

Several more specialised cases were also available for various medical officers and specialists to carry the materials and tools of their trade. These were made of black or brown leather with lid tops and a fixed leather hand-carrying strap. They included the doctor's case (*Arzttasche*), dentist's case (*Zahnarztasche*), pharmacist's case (*Apothekertasche*), and veterinarian's case (*Veterinärtasche*), the latter of which could be mounted on the saddle.

Some medical orderlies were issued a **refreshment flask** (*Labeflasche*) similar to the model issued to mountain troops. The medical troops' model was of 1.5 litre (about 50 ounce) capacity

A cavalry squad in France, 1940, displays the M1934 saddle bags. Even though replaced by the new type saddle bags in 1940, the M1934 remained in more common use throughout the war. (US Army)

and was of the same basic design as the mountain troops, including the securing strap and cup. However, there was no carrying attachment hook, but rather a leather shoulder strap that buckled to a vertical strap fastened around the flask's bottom, running up the edges and attached to a horizontal strap fastened around its circumference. The carrying strap was worn over the left shoulder and the flask carried at the right hip or rear. Production of this item ceased in about 1943.

Miscellaneous equipment

The **report pouch** (*Meldtasche*) was a small black leather case secured by a snap-closed flap. It was carried by the reporting NCO ('*der Spiess*' — slang term) of company-sized units, roughly equivalent to a US first sergeant. In it were stored blank unit daily strength report forms, unit rosters, and a pen or pencil. It was traditionally tucked in the front of the reporting NCO's tunic between the second and third buttons, as it had no belt attachments.

The **musician's pouch** (*Musikertasche*) was issued to bandsmen to carry sheet music, extra mouthpieces and reeds for woodwind instruments, and cleaning materials. Made of black leather, its flap was closed by a buckle-secured strap. Two leather loops were fitted to the back permitting it to be worn on the left front of the waist belt.

THE PLATES

(*Note:* When identifying items attached to belts in a laid-out display, the order of description is from the reader's left to right.)

A: Infantryman's Equipment, 1939–40

A1: A rifleman's equipment at the outbreak of war included the belt supports with auxiliary straps, leather belt and buckle, M1911 cartridge pouches, small entrenching tool and carrier, S84/98 bayonet and dismounted sidearm carrier (frog), M1930 gas mask case with gas sheet on the shoulder strap, M1931 bread bag, and M1931 field flask and drinking cup. These items served as the basis for other combat troops' equipment.

A2: Austrian spade for infantrymen with carrier, S84/98 bayonet, and sidearm carrier; used by Austrian units inducted into the German Army.

A3: Variant of the M1931 bread bag with its little-used shoulder strap.

A4: Upper—Web pack frame of the combat pack for infantry rifle companies attached to the belt supports with auxiliary straps.

A4: Lower—Combat pack, without belt supports, with typical items attached, upper to lower. M1931 cook pot, M1931 tent quarter (dark side), and bag for combat pack.

A5: M1939 pack showing the interior flaps and a greatcoat strap for foot troops.

A6: M1934 pack with integral shoulder straps.

B: Infantryman's and Troop Leader's Equipment, 1939–41

B1: This 28th Inf. Regt., 8th Inf. Div. MG34 machine gunner is outfitted with typical equipment: belt supports with auxiliary straps, leather belt and buckle, M1934 repair parts pouch, P08 pistol holster with Luger, small entrenching tool and carrier, M1938 gas mask case with gas sheet reversed (to limit bouncing) on the shoulder strap, M1931 bread bag, and M1931 field flask. An M1934 spare barrel carrier is slung across his back, and an issue field pocket lamp is attached to a tunic button.

B2: M1931 tent quarter showing the light camouflage pattern side.

B3: An open M1931 bread bag.

B4: M1931 clothing bag.

B5: Tent accessory bag, one of many variants, this one with securing straps.

B6: Sauer M38(H) pistol holster, typical of most 7.65mm handgun holsters.

B7: M1935 report/map case, one of many common variants.

B8: M1934 officer's belt with shoulder strap. Attached is a full-flap M1935 report/map case variant, and a Walther PPK pistol holster as used by many senior and rear area officers.

B9: Standard issue universal 6 × 30 binoculars with leather container and eyepiece protector.

C: Tropical Equipment, 1940–42

C1: An ideal set of rifleman's equipment in North Africa (though mixed tropical and Continental gear was more common) was fabricated almost entirely of canvas and webbing with little use of leather. Metal items were painted reed green, sand colour, or tan, as were sometimes Continental issue leather items. It included the web tropical belt supports for infantry, web tropical belt and buckle, tropical leather cartridge pouches (much more common were standard black leather pouches), small entrenching tool and tropical carrier, S84/98 bayonet and tropical sidearm carrier, M1938 gas mask case with tropical gas sheet on the shoulder strap, tropical bread bag, and two tropical field flasks. This same basic design of equipment, often in olive green and tan, was issued Army-wide from 1943.

C2: Tropical rifle grenade launcher pouch with 3cm cup-type launcher.

C3: Canvas large signal cartridge pouch for the flare pistol; also used on the Continent.

C4: Tropical MP38/MP40 machine pistol magazine pouches.

C5: A combat unit officer's little-used web tropical belt and buckle, with tan-painted leather belt support straps for officers (formerly, 'support straps for cartridge pouches'), early model Walther P38 pistol holster, tan-painted leather M1935 despatch/map case variant, and variant tropical field flask with phenolic resin covering attached to an inverted supplementary loop.

C6: Web combat pack frame, with tropical belt supports and typical items attached—upper to lower: tropical cook pot

The back of a right side M1934 saddle bag displaying the shoulder straps enabling it to be used as a backpack by dismounted cavalrymen. (Troy Haley collection)

ropical tent quarter, and bag for the combat pack.

C7: Battle rucksack, a version used in North Africa, with a tropical greatcoat strap.

D: Specialist Equipment, 1939–45

D1: Pioneer assault pack assembly fastened to a standard belt and belt supports for infantry (formerly, 'belt supports with auxiliary straps'). Equipment includes a hand grenade side pouch with M1924 stick, M1939 smoke stick, and M1939 'egg' hand grenades; S84/98 bayonet and mounted sidearm carrier; assault pouch with (from top to bottom) cook pot, NbK39 smoke pot, and 3kg demolition charge compartments; M1931 field flask attached to an inverted supplementary loop; and rubber-lined demolition charge and gas mask side pouch with an M1928 100g boring cartridge, and M1928 200g and M1924 1kg demolition charges, along with an M1938 gas mask. Beside it is a pioneer spade, with detachable blade, and carrier.

D2: Rucksack for artillery; standard model with integral shoulder straps.

D3: M1934 medical pack.

D4: Model 2 radio pack.

D5: Holster for the 2.7cm signal pistol with long barrel.

D6: Leather large signal cartridge pouch for 18 rounds.

D7: Leather small signal cartridge pouch for 12 rounds with 2.7cm cartridges.

D8: Pair of dismounted medical pouches.

D9: Refreshment flask (1.5 litre) used by medical personnel.

A cavalryman's Kar.98k carbine carried in the carbine shoe. Behind the saddle's cantle is the rear baggage roll. (US Army)

Signalmen attach a field telephone to a telephone line. All wearing the tent quarter as a weather cape. (Author's collection)

D10: M1939 carrying harness for M1936 5cm light mortar components. A bag for the combat pack was issued with it and attached at the frame's top.

E: Mounted Troops Equipment, 1939–45

(Note: The saddle bags are oriented as though the horse's head is to the top of the page.)

E1: A cavalryman's equipment early in the war included the belt supports for cavalry (previously, 'cavalry supports'), leather belt and buckle, M1911 cartridge pouches, S84/98 bayonet and mounted sidearm carrier, carbine holder sling, M1931 field flask attached to an inverted supplementary loop, and M1938 gas mask case (positioned for mounted wear).

E2: Carbine shoe, attached to the saddle when used in conjunction with the carbine holder sling fastened to the waist belt, together forming the carbine holding device.

E3: New type saddle bags, adopted in 1940.

E4: M1934 saddle bags.

E5: M1926 saddle bags.

E6: Old type saddle bags.

F: Mountain Troops Equipment, 1939–45

F1: Mountain infantrymen in the early war years (here, 1940, 98th Mt. Inf. Regt., 1st Mt. Div.) used both specialised and standard issue equipment. As the war progressed the supply system deteriorated, and the mountain troops were more often committed to battle as conventional infantry; their specialised equipment and uniforms now began to resemble other

An MP40 machine pistol armed squad leader with olive green early model magazine pouches. This model was issued in North Africa in reed green. Note that the support straps for infantry are attached to supplementary loops on the belt rather than the pouches' 'D' rings. (US Army)

A squad leader's equipment typically was configured with support straps for infantry, belt, late model MP40 machine pistol magazine pouches (olive green), small entrenching tool and carrier, M1931 bread bag, and M1931 field flask. (Troy Haley collection)

A late war rifleman's equipment might consist of web (olive green) support straps for infantry, belt, M1911 cartridge pouches, S.84/98 bayonet, folding spade and carrier, M1931 bread bag (dark tan), and M1931 field flask. (Troy Haley collection)

infantrymen's. Mountain equipment includes the special tinted goggles, M1931 rucksack for high mountain troops with an M1938 gas mask case attached, large flask for mountain troops, ice axe (used only by high mountain troops), and a Gew.33/40 carbine (former Czechoslovak vz.16/33), modified for mountain troops.

F2: Flask for mountain troops (1 litre).

F3: Modified wartime production M1931 mountain rucksack.

F4: Medical rucksack, front and back. It was attached to infantry support straps. This model was also used as a battle rucksack without the red cross patch.

F5: Variant battle rucksack used by mountain and infantry units, with integral shoulder straps.

G: Infantry Equipment, 1942–44

G1: Late in the war it was not unusual for riflemen's equipment especially within security, training and replacement units, to include captured and impounded items. This set lacks belt support straps (common in rear areas and support units), but includes a leather belt and buckle, a single Polish cartridge pouch (for Wz.24 carbine, identical to Kar.98k), Polish entrenching tool and carrier, S84/98 bayonet and late war sidearm carrier (also made entirely in webbing), late type M1938 gas mask case (adopted in late 1941) with a gas cape attached by unauthorised rubber bands, late war M1931 bread bag, and late war M1931 field flask.

G2: A Panzergrenadier of the 76th Pz. Gren. Regt., 20th Pz

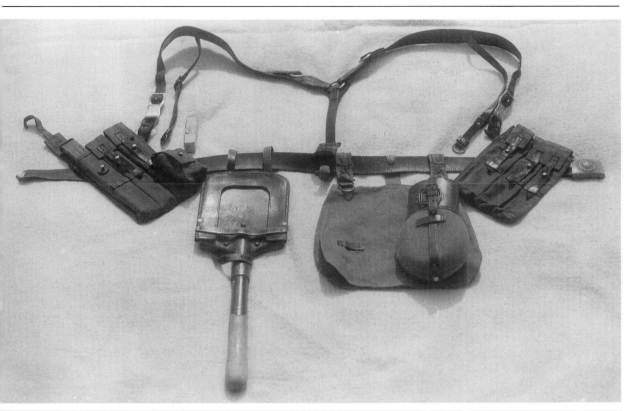

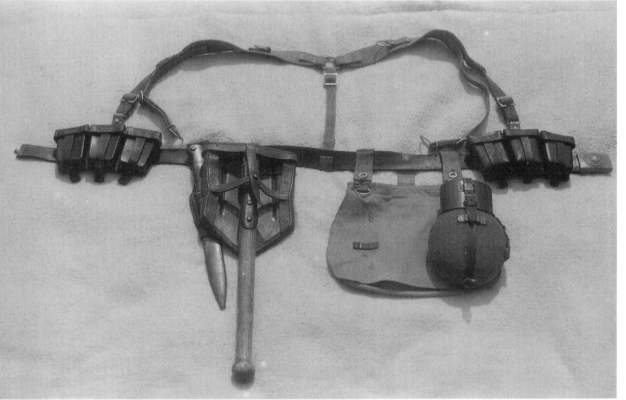

These Pz.Kpfw. IV tank crewmen have erected a standard configuration four-man tent, using four tent quarter sections, on a rail flatcar, mid-1943. The light camouflage side is showing. (Author's collection)

Gren. Div., 1944, equipped with belt supports for cavalry (often used by other than cavalry units), leather belt and buckle, early issue MP43 machine pistol magazine pouches, folding spade and early model carrier, late type M1938 gas mask container, late war bread bag, and late war field flask. He is armed with an MP43 machine pistol (assault rifle).

G3: An open late-war bread bag with the M1934 carbine cleaning kit pocket added in late 1944. The shoulder strap fittings had been eliminated earlier.

G4: Late model MP38/40 machine pistol magazine pouches.

G5: Late model Walther P38 pistol holster, used from late 1943.

G6: Early leather rifle grenade launcher pouch with detachable strap.

G7: Carrying pouches for rifle grenades with 3cm anti-tank and anti-personnel rifle grenades.

G8: Metal carrying case for the Zf41 (1.5 power) telescope (*Zielfernrohr*) for the Kar.98k, one of the more common of many models. This model was issued to selected riflemen rather than trained snipers, who received more powerful scopes. Early versions of this case were painted olive green and had a black leather belt strap.

H: Infantry Equipment, 1943–45

H1: A late war Grenadier's equipment might include the web belt supports for infantry, web belt and late war buckle, Gew.43 self-loading weapon magazine pouches, folding spade and late model carrier, late type M1938 gas mask case with gas sheet, late war bread bag, M1931 cook pot, field flask, and M1911 cartridge pouches. He is armed with a Gew.43 self-loading rifle, *Panzerfaust* 60 anti-tank rocket launcher, and M1943 stick hand grenade.

H2: Late war rucksack for artillery designed for attaching to belt supports for infantry, and issued to cyclists and some infantry units.

H3: Pair of carrying bags for rifle grenades with a 6.1cm GG/P.40 anti-tank grenade.

H4: Late war *Press-Stoff* rifle grenade pouch with permanently attached shoulder strap, and a spigot-type launcher and folding sight for the GG/P.40.

H5: Late war assault rifle magazine pouches for the StG44 (formerly MP44) assault rifle.

H6: SA bread bag, used by the Army as a limited substitute.

H7: The same equipment as worn by H1 displayed: web belt supports for infantry (with the back strap attached to a supplementary loop to accommodate a tall individual), web belt and late war buckle, Gew.43 self-loading weapon magazine pouches, folding spade and late model carrier, late type M1938 gas mask case with gas sheet attached in the authorised manner, late war bread bag, M1931 cook pot, late war field flask with a phenolic resin covering, and M1911 cartridge pouches.

Notes sur les planches en couleur

A1 Equipement de fusilier, comprenant des supports de ceinturon, un ceinturon de cuir avec boucle, des cartouchières, des outils de tranchée avec sac, une baïonnette et un porte-baïonnette, un masque à gaz et un voile, un sac à pain, une gourde et un gobelet de combat. **A2** Pelle autrichienne avec étui, baïonnette et portebaïonnette, comme ceux utilisés par les unités autrichiennes enrôlées dans l'armée allemande. **A3** Variante du sac à pain avec bandoulière M1931. **A4** En haut – Armature d'un sac de toile faisant partie d'un sac à dos de combat d'infanterie. En bas – Sac à dos de combat avec objets caractéristiques attachés. **A5** Sac à dos M1934. **A6** Sac à dos M1934 avec courroies intégrales pour les épaules.

B1 Equipement caractéristique de mitrailleur: supports de ceinturon avec courroies auxiliaires, ceinturon de cuir avec boucle, sac contenant des pièces détachées, étui de pistolet avec Luger, petit outil de tranchée avec étui, boîte pour masque à gaz avec un voile renversé sur la courroie de l'épaule, sac à pain et gourde de combat. Ils transportaient également un étui de canon de fusil de réserve et une lampe de poche de combat. **B2** Quart de tente M1931. **B3** Sac à pain M1931. **B4** Sac à vêtements M1931. **B5** Sac à accessoires de tente. **B6** Etui de pistolet Sauer M38(H). **B7** Etui de rapport/carte. **B8** Ceinture d'officier M1934. Un étui de rapport/carte et un étui de pistolet Walther PPk y sont attachés. **B9** Jumelles standard avec étui en cuir et protège-oculaires.

C1 Un équipement de fusilier en Afrique du Nord, comprenant supports de ceinturon, ceinturon et boucle, cartouchières, outil de tranchée avec étui, boîte à masque à gaz et voile, sac à pain et deux gourdes pour le champ de bataille. **C2** Etui lance-grenades à fusil avec lance-grenades, type à coupelle de 3cm. **C3** Gros étui à fusées de signalisation pour pistolet lance-fusées. **C4** Sacs à poudrière caractéristiques MP38/MP40. **C5** Ceinturon et boucle appartenant à un officier d'unité de combat, courroies pour supports de ceinturon, étui à pistolet Walther P38, étui pour documents à expédier/cartes, et gourde pour le champ de bataille. **C6** Armature de sac à dos de combat en toile avec supports de ceinturon et casserole, quart de tente et sac pour équipement de combat attachés. **C7** Version nord-africaine d'un sac à dos de bataille.

D1 Sac à dos d'assaut d'une éclaireur avec porte-grenades latéral de grenade à main et grenades, baïonnette avec porte-baïonnette, sac d'assaut, gourde pour le champ de bataille et une charge de démolition recouverte d'une pellicule de caoutchouc et étui de masque à gaz. A côté se trouve une pelle pour éclaireur avec plat détachable et étui. **D2** Sac à dos d'artillerie. **D3** Trousse médicale M1934. **D4** Ensemble radio modèle 2. **D5** Etui de pistolet lance-fusées de 2,7 cm avec long barillet. **D6** Grande cartouchière à fusées de signalisation pour 18 coups. **D7** Petite cartouchière à fusées de signalisation pour 12 coups. **D8** Paire de trousses médicales démontées. **D9** Gourde de rafraîchissement pour le personnel médical. **D10** Harnais M1939 pour pièces de 5 cm de mortier léger M1939.

E1 Ancien modèle d'équipement de cavalier, comprenant supports de ceinturon, ceinturon et boucle, cartouchières, baïonnette et porte-baïonnette, bandoulière de carabine, gourde de combat et boîte de masque à gaz. **E2** Bourrelet de renforcement pour carabine utilisé avec bandoulière de carabine. **E3** Nouveau modèle de sacoches de selle. **E4** Sacoche de selle M1934. **E5** Sacoches de selle M1926. **E6** Sacoche de selle de modèle ancien.

F1 Ancien modèle d'équipement de fantassin montagnard, comprenant lunettes protectrices teintées, sac à dos, boîte pour masque à gaz, grosse gourde, scie à glace et carabine Gew.33/40. **F2** Gourde pour troupes de montagnes. **F3** Sac à dos de montagne modifié M1931. **F4** Sac à dos médical. **F5** Variante de sac à dos de bataille.

G1 Equipement d'infanterie datant de la fin de la guerre, sans supports de ceinturon, mais avec ceinturon et boucle, cartouchière polonaise pour une seule cartouche, outil de tranchée polonais avec étui, baïonnette et porte-baïonnette, boîte de masque à gaz, cape à gaz, sac à pain et gourde de combat. **G2** Un Panzergrenadier (1944) avec supports de ceinturon de cavalerie, ceinturon et boucle, sacs à poudrière MP43 de modèle ancien, pelle pliante et étui, conteneur de masques à gaz, sac à pain et gourde de combat. Il est armé d'une mitrailleuse MP43. **G3** Sac à pain de la fin de la guerre avec sac nécessaire pour nettoyer les carabines. **G4** Modèle plus récent de sacs à poudrière MP38/40. **G5** Modèle plus récent d'étui à pistolet Walther P38. **G6** Etui à fusil lance-grenades de modèle ancien. **G7** Etuis à fusils lance-grenades. **G8** Boîte en métal servant à transporter le fusil téléscopique Kar 98k.

H1 Equipement de grenadierm modèle fin de la guerre, comprenant supports de ceinturon en toile, ceinturon de toile et modèle de boucle de la fin de la guerre, sacs à poudrière Gew.43, pelle pliante et étui, boître de masque à gaz et voile, sac à pain, casserole, gourde de combat et cartouchières. Il est armé d'un fusil automatique Gew.43, d'un Panzerfaust 60 et d'une grenade à manche. **H2** Sac à dos pour artillerie, modèle de fin de la guerre. **H3** Sacs pour porter les grenades à fusil avec grenade anti-char de 6,1 cm GG/P.40. **H4** Etui à grenade pour fusil Press-Stoff, lance-grenades de type tuyau et visée repliable pour le GG/P40. **H5** Sacs à poudrière pour fusil d'assaut STG44. **H6** Sac à pain 5A. **H7** Même équipement que H1, supports de toile, ceinturon de toile et boucle, sacs à poudrière Gew.43, pelle pliante et étui, boîte de masque à gaz et voile, sac à pain, casserole, gourde de combat et cartouchières.

Farbtafeln

A1 Zur Ausrüstung eines Schützen gehörten Gürtelriemen, Ledergürtel und Schnalle, Patronentaschen, Schaufel samt Tragvorrichtung, Bajonett samt Tragvorrichtung. Gasmaskenbehälter mit Tuch, Brotbeutel, Feldflasche und Trinkbecher. **A2** Österreichischer Spaten und Tragvorrichtung, Bajonett und Tragvorrichtung, wie üblich bei österreichischen Einheiten in der deutschen Armee. **A3** Variante des M1931-Brotbeutel mit Schulterriemen. **A4** Oben – Infanterie-Gürtelranzen mit Riemen. Unten – Gürtelranzen mit typischem Zubehör. **A5** M1939-Gürtelranzen. **A6** M1934-Ranzen mit integrierten Schulterriemen.

B1 Typische MG-Schützenausrüstung: Gürtelriemen mit Zusatzriemen, Ledergürtel mit Schnalle, Ersatzteilbeutel, Pistolenhalfter mit Luger, kleiner Spaten mit Tragvorrichtung, Gasmaskenbehälter mit Schutztuch an Schulterriemen, Brotbeutel und Feldflasche. Ebenfalls mitgetragen: Behälter für Ersatzlauf für MG und Taschenlampe. **B2** M1931-Zeltteil. **B3** M1931-Brotbeutel. **B4** M1931-Kleiderbehälter. **B5** Zeltzubehörbeutel. **B6** Sauer M38 (H)-Pistolenhalfter. **B7** M1935-Report/Landkartenmappe. **B8** M1934-Offiziersgürtel mit Report/Landkartenmappe und Walther PPk-Pistolenhalfter. **B9** Standard-feldstecher mit Lederbehälter und Okularschützer.

C1 Ausrüstung eines Schützen in Nordafrika mit Gürtelriemen, Gürtel und Schnalle, Patronentaschen, Spaten mit Tragvorrichtung, Gasmaskenbehälter mit Schutztuch, Brotbeutel und zwei Feldflaschen. **C2** Granatwerferranzen mit 3 cm Becherwerfer. **C3** Ranzen für große Leuchtpatronen für Leuchtpistole. **C4** Typische MP38/MP40-Magazinbehälter. **C5** Gürtelausrüstung eines Offiziers einer Einsatztruppe, mit Gürtel und Schnalle, Gürtelriemen, Halfter für Walther P38, Aktenmappe und Feldflasche. **C6** Gürtelranzen mit Gürtelriemen und Kochtopf, Zeltteil und Sack für Gürtelranzen. **C7** Nordafrikanische Version eines Feldrucksacks.

D1 Pionier-Kampffranzen mit Handgranatentasche und Granaten, Bajonett samt Tragvorrichtung, Kampffranzen, Feldflasche und gummigefütterter Behälter für Sprengladung und Gasmaske. Daneben Pionierspaten mit abnehmbarer Schaufel samt Tragvorrichtung. **D2** Artilleristen-Rucksack. **D3** M1934-Sanitäterranzen. **D4** Funkgerät-Ranzen Modell 2. **D5** Halfter für 2,7 cm Leuchtpistole mit langem Lauf. **D6** Großer Leuchtpatronensack für 18 Patronen. **D7** Kleiner Leuchtpatronensack für 12 Patronen. **D8** Ein Paar separater Sanitäterranzen. **D9** Feldflasche für Sanitäter. **D10** M1939-Tragvorrichtung für M1939-Leichtmörserteile.

E1 Frühe Kavalleristenausrüstung mit Gürtelriemen, Gürtel und Schnalle, Patronentaschen, Bajonett und Halfter, Karabinergurt, Feldflasche und Gasmaskenbehälter. **E2** Karabinerbehälter mit Karabinergurt. **E3** Neuartige Satteltaschen. **E6** Alte Satteltaschen.

F1 Frühe Gebirgsjägerausrüstung mit Sonnenbrillen, Rucksack, Gasmaskenbehälter, großer Feldflasche, Eispickel und Karabiner Gew.33/40. **F2** Feldflasche für Gebirgstruppen. **F3** Modifizierter M1931-Rucksack. **F4** Sanitäter-Rucksack. **F5** Variante eines Kampfrucksacks.

G1 Infanterieausrüstung gegen Kriegsende, ohne Gürtelriemen, aber mit Gürtel und Schnalle, einer polnischen Patronentasche, einem polnischen Spaten mit Halfter, Bajonett und Halfter, Gasmaskenbehälter, Gasschutzumhang, Brotbeutel und Feldflasche. **G2** Ein Panzergrenadier (1944) mit Kavallerie-Gürtelriemen, Gürtel mit Schnalle, frühe MP43-Magazintaschen, faltbarer Spaten mit Halfter, Gasmaskenbehälter, Brotbeutel und Feldflasche. Bewaffnet mit MP43-Maschinenpistole. **G3** Brotbeutel gegen Kriegsende, mit Tasche für Karabiner-Reinigungszeug. **G4** Spätes Modell von MP38/40-Magazintaschen. **G5** Spätes Modell eines Walther P38-Pistolenhalfters. **G6** Frühe Granatwerfertasche. **G7** Granatentaschen. **G8** Metallkasten für KAR 98K-Zielfernrohr.

H1 Grenadierausrüstung gegen Kriegsende, mit Gürtelriemen, Gürtel und später Schnalle, Gew.43-Munitionstaschen, faltbarer Spaten mit Halfter, M1938-Gasmaskenbehälter, Brotbeutel, Kochtopf, Feldflasche und Patronentaschen. Bewaffnet mit einem automatischen Gew.43-Gewehr, einem Panzerfaust 60 und einer M1943-Handgranate. **H2** Später Artilleristen-Rucksack. **H3** Tragsäcke für Granaten, mit einer 6,1 cm GG/P.40-Panzerabwehrgranate. **H4** Press-Stoff-Gewehrgranatensack Granatwerfer und Faltvisier für GG/P40. **H5** Patronentaschen für STG44-Gewehr. **H6** 5A-Brotbeutel. **H7** Wie H1. Gürtelriemen, Gürtel und Schnalle, Gew.43-Munitionstaschen, Faltspaten samt Halfter, Gasmaskenbehälter, Gasmaskenschutztuch, Brotbeutel, Kochtopf, Feldflasche und Patronentaschen.